The Ultimate Playlist

THE 100
Greatest
COVER
versions

Rober...

Published by McNidder & Grace
4 Chapel Lane, Alnwick, NE66 1XT

First Published 2012

© Robert Webb

A catalogue record for this work is available from the British Library.

ISBN: 978-0-85716-019-5

Designed by Obsidian Design

Printed by Short Run Press Ltd, Exeter

To Kathy, Barney and Arthur

ACKNOWLEDGEMENTS

Some of the pieces in this book first appeared, in one shape or another, in the *Independent* between 2001 and 2010, in my columns *Story of the Song* and *Double Take*.

I am indebted to the many singers and songwriters, too numerous to mention individually, who, over the years, have explained how (and why) they wrote and recorded some of their best-known songs. I am, as ever, immeasurably grateful for the encouragement and support of my wonderful wife, Kathy, who has had to endure my record collection for longer than is probably healthy. Thanks are also due especially to Andrew Peden Smith at McNidder & Grace. For ideas, inspiration and all-round encouragement I am grateful to Mark Narayn, Mollie Narayn, Louis Narayn, Laurie Staff, Nick Coleman, Derek Chapman, Richard Balls, Jem Bailey and Tim Allen. Appreciation also to Dorothy Howe and Adam White. And last, but not least, to my mother, Jean Webb, with whom I heard my first memorable cover version (Millie's 'My Boy Lollipop').

Robert Webb

2012

Contents

x

INTRODUCTION

Which Blondie Top Five was originally a flop for a West Coast power pop band? Who wrote Alice Cooper's 1973 hit 'Hello Hurray', and which folk singer first recorded it? Who launched their career with a tear and a cover of a little known Prince song? Where was Joe Cocker sitting when he came up with the idea of covering 'With a Little Help from my Friends?'

The 100 Greatest Cover Versions traces the histories of some of the great songs you may know only as second-hand recordings and explores some unusual and creative takes on a few of pop's well-known tracks. First though, an admission. I imagine that not all the songs in this book will be on your own list of "great cover versions" and, in truth, several are not on mine. There is an intended irony and deliberate provocation in the book's title – yes, I know, the whole thing is meaninglessly subjective anyway. But, stepping back, I can't in all honesty defend them all as amongst "the greatest". ('Mony Mony' is a feelgood number, for sure, but, on reflection, Billy Idol's version is perhaps not a champion cover. Someone out there must really like it, though: it was a huge hit.) So, where the remake isn't "great" in a critical sense (whatever that might mean), I would argue the original is, hence its inclusion in this book. Most importantly, though, my criterion is that the backstory is worth retelling. And everybody likes a good song – and a good story.

A great song will travel and plenty of artists have more than a few covers in their back catalogue. Some have even assembled whole albums of borrowed songs.

By the early Seventies, as pop began to glance over its shoulder to see where it had come from, the idea of dipping into a gene pool of popular song became rather an attractive one. David Bowie, Bryan Ferry and The Band all released albums in 1973 comprising other people's songs, exhumed from the previous decade and a half. Those long players – Bowie's especially, called *Pin Ups* – now slot seamlessly into the eclecticism of the early Seventies, but at the time Bowie was at the avant-garde of pop, a forward-thrusting, chameleon-coloured modernist, and it seemed an odd move. The shock of the old, perhaps?

In truth the quixotic *Pin Ups* and Ferry's *These Foolish Things* were nothing more than exercises in thumbing through the musical photo album to point, misty-eyed, at their roots, before the two bright young things moved on to the next phase of their respective, ever-shifting futures. Both records were hugely successful and helped pave the way towards a trend for tribute albums in the decades that followed.

The same year (1973), Harry Nilsson, something of a cover version king, took the concept one step further (back), issuing *A Little Touch of Schmilsson in the Night*, his entirely un-rocking, orchestrated croon through the great American songbook (and an immeasurable improvement on Ringo Starr's own similarly old-timer set, *Sentimental Journey*). Also in '73 John Lennon began work on *Rock 'n' roll*, a tribute to his own formative period – whilst taking time out to collaborate on parboiled covers set with Nilsson, the lovingly confused *Pussy Cats*.

The Band's *Moondog Matinee*, in which they resurrect some pet sounds from the Fifties, came about largely though a lack of any real original ideas. As Levon Helm, the band's drummer, recalled: someone suggested, "why don't we just do our old nightclub act?" Their retread of Fats Domino, Chuck Berry and Elvis standards was met with little critical sympathy at the time, but the album brought some great songs back to life and cast them at a new, younger audience. It's since been the subject of some revisionist thinking – in 2010, Rhapsody radio, declared The Band's version of 'Mystery Train' to be "crisp, funky and ready for a barroom brawl to break out".

By the Nineties the single-artist covers albums was *de rigueur* in new pop. Nick Cave and the Bad Seeds' *Kicking Against the Pricks* (1986) boots the bottom out of some unlikely hand-me-downs from the likes of Glen Campbell, Gene Pitney and the Seekers. The following year, Siouxsie and the Banshees issued *Through the Looking Glass*, on which they name-check some of their pre-punk heroes (Sparks, John Cale, Kraftwerk, Television, and so on).

Elvis Costello followed up his 1981 album of country covers, *Almost Blue*, with an early-Nineties round-up of some of his personal favourites from rock, country and R&B, *Kojak Variety*, which sequences some Kitemark covers of the Kinks, Jesse Winchester and Little Richard, amongst others. Ironically, despite being one of the late-twentieth century's great songwriters, Costello's biggest chart hits, like Nilsson's, have largely been with other people's songs ('A Good Year for the Roses', 'I Can't Stand up for Falling Down' and 'She').

Duran Duran even weighed in with *Thank You* (1995), a covers collection finds the Birmingham beatsters tackling songs like Bob Dylan's 'Lay Lady Lay' (incidentally, originally pitched by Dylan as the theme for *Midnight Cowboy*, but losing out to Nilsson and his appropriation of Fred Neil's world-go-away anthem 'Everybody's Talking'), Costello's 'Watching the Detectives' and truly execrable, middle England covers of Grandmaster Melle Mel's 'White Lines (Don't do it)' and the Temptation's 'Ball of Confusion'. No, thank you. It's difficult to see who, exactly, the album was aimed at.

As the new millennium curved into view, Paul McCartney replicated Lennon's *Rock 'n' roll* outing with a retro collection of his own, *Run Devil Run*, where – alongside guest musicians such as David Gilmore, Dave Mattacks and Pete Wingfield – Macca lovingly recreates his musical youth.

The funk-ball that is Mark Ronson's *Version*, issued in 2007, brought a fresh approach to the genre by revving up material from the Kaiser Chiefs, Paul Weller and others. With a roster of contemporary, radio-friendly singers on board, it broke the covers-album mould by looking defiantly forward, rather than back, and thus spawning the Amy Winehouse hit 'Valerie'. Another of the decade's more idiosyncratic covers albums was Peter Gabriel's *Scratch My Back*, one half of a planned project – the anticipated follow-up, *You Scratch Mine*, is supposedly a saddlebag of Gabriel songs covered by others (some have already been released as iTunes exclusives). Less original was Gabriel's ex-bandmate Phil Collins' slick collection of copycat Motown covers, *Going Back*: respectful, but lacking soul.

Rumer's bittersweet 2012 covers album, *Boys Don't Cry*, cuddles up with some of pop's more overlooked songwriters, including Todd Rundgren, Ronnie Lane, Gilbert O'Sullivan, Terry Reid and Clifford T. Ward.

The cult of the cover has inevitably spawned numerous blogspots and forums, where listeners and completists can jostle, argue and proffer playlists of their own. Some songs are so cover friendly that they have deservedly been granted their own scholarly website – notably summertime-connection.nl, devoted to the apparently (and astonishing) 33,000-plus-and-counting recorded versions of Gershwin's 'Summertime' (although surely not all commercially released? I can only find 48 on Spotify). Sam Cooke's will do it for me.

So here is my selection of 100 cover versions. Many can be heard on Spotify or downloaded from your favourite online store. Others you will have to rip from CD in order to compile that perfect playlist. Some you may have to search a little harder for.

I apologise if your personal favourite isn't included (although perhaps not, if it is one of the estimated three thousand released versions of the overrated 'Yesterday'). But here's your chance to pitch in. Follow us @100covers or visit the website at www. ultimateplaylists.co.uk to post your own playlist and tell the world why disco versions of Pink Floyd and Neil Young shouldn't be allowed, why you think Kate Bush's 1991 cover of Elton John's 'Rocket Man (I Think it's Going to Be a Long, Long Time)' (voted by *Observer* readers as the greatest cover of all time in 2007) is a criminal omission – or why Billy Idol's 'Mony Mony' really is great.

LOUIE LOUIE
THE KINGSMEN (1963)
Original by Richard Berry (1956)

It's the ultimate garage anthem: so good they named it twice. There are well-known versions by Iggy Pop, the Kinks, Motorhead and the Flamin' Groovies and even one by Julie 'Cry Me a River' London. One source has documented over a thousand recorded versions of 'Louie Louie'. There are books and blogs devoted to its convoluted history and there's even an album, *Love That Louie: The Louie Louie Files*, a compilation of 24 of the best versions. Not bad for a two-minute riff which started out as a lowly, neglected B-side.

The earliest version we usually hear is by the Kingsmen. First recorded with Jack Ely on vocals, the mix featured on the band's 1963 album *In Person* was overdubbed with audience noise to create a "live" feel. The original undubbed recording made it to seven-inch in 1966 and has been widely anthologised.

'Louie Louie' was already seven years old in 1963. It was written by Richard Berry, a Louisiana-born singer who toured rock 'n' roll and doo-wop covers at weekends with an LA outfit called the Rhythm Rockers, often performing two shows a night. Berry tended to sit out the first part of the set, which was largely instrumental. As Dave Marsh explains in the book *Louie Louie*, one night Berry heard a steady pulse thrumming through the dressing-room walls: *duh-duh-duh, duh duh*. The song being played on stage was Rene Touzet's arrangement of 'Amarren Al Loco', retitled 'El Loco Cha Cha'. The beat was hardly new in Latin music but, thanks to the muffled acoustics in the dressing room, Berry was transfixed. Keeping the rhythmic cadence in his head, he scribbled down some lyrics about a homesick sailor and a barkeeper. He dissected the cha-cha chug and assembled a Latin-infused R&B number.

In Berry's song, the sailor has no name, but the barkeeper does: Louie.

It was April 1956 and Berry needed some material for an upcoming session of his own: that would do nicely. Later that year Flip Records issued a single by Richard Berry and the Pharaohs, with his new song, 'Louie Louie', on the flip. The B-side was good, but people seemed to prefer the A-side, 'You are my Sunshine'. "I didn't think 'Louie Louie' was gonna be a hit," said Berry. "I just thought it was a good song that I wrote." Eventually listeners came around to 'Louie Louie', making it a regional hit of sorts. But pop quickly moved on and Berry's record was mostly forgotten within months.

It was Ron Holden and the Playboys who first revived the dormant 'Louie Louie', in the late Fifties, initially for the Pacific northwest's growing garage-band scene. Then it was the Wailers' turn to record it. Then a dozen more bands. By the time the Kingsmen got a hold of it, 'Louie Louie' was no longer a Latin groove – it was rock 'n' roll. And so great was it that the Kingsmen once played an hour-and-a-half set riffing on just the one song: 90 minutes, *duh-duh-duh, duh duh*.

IT'S ALL OVER NOW
THE ROLLING STONES (1964)
Original by the Valentinos (1964)

With three British hit singles behind them and a bad reputation, the Rolling Stones found themselves in Chicago's Chess Studios, trying to crack America. Chess was where their heroes Muddy Waters and Chuck Berry cut some of the quintet's favourite tracks and this, decided their swaggering, 20-year-old manager Andrew Loog Oldham, who'd flown them over on a wing and a prayer, was where the Stones would make their name.

In the summer of 1964 'It's All Over Now' had just been released by brotherly R&B-soul outfit the Valentinos. The Stones first heard this rousing girl-done-me-wrong number, which came from the pen of the Valentinos' principal songwriter Bobby Womack, during the course of a radio interview with legendary DJ Murray the K. It was leapt upon by Oldham and the boys, who wasted no time in blagging recording rights for the Chess session. At first Womack was less than happy at having his song probably ruined by a bunch of lanky Brits. "I didn't want the Rolling Stones to record that song," he recalled. "It was so important for that record to happen for the Valentinos."

Womack soon found the flood of royalties eased the pain. It was released in Britain to advance orders of 150,000 – backed with the promise of having actually been made in America. The Stones transformed 'It's All Over Now' from a ballsy soul groove into an early rock classic. Keith's guitar grunts at Brian's jaunty, country-style finger-picking. Jagger's vocals snipe back. The Stones swept the charts with it, providing the young punks with their first Number One. The Valentinos' original, by contrast, turned out to be their final chart appearance, reaching a lowly Number 94 in the US. It nevertheless gave Womack the recognition he deserved as one of soul's primary singer-songwriters.

SAILING
ROD STEWART (1975)
Original by the Sutherland Brothers (1972)

Rod Stewart's glasspaper tonsils have smoothed and shaped songs by, amongst others, Tom Waits, Jimi Hendrix and Cat Stevens. None has quite the gravitas of its original (although his take on Crazy Horse's 'I Don't Want to Talk About It' was his last truly great single). The first cut, invariably, is the deepest. 1975's 'Sailing' was Rod's third British Number One and the first cover he really made his own. It was first recorded by the Aberdeenshire two-piece Gavin and Iain Sutherland in 1972 – the Proclaimers of their day, who later teamed up with the pub rock band Quiver. Although awarded a fair bit of after-dark airtime, there was no chart action.

Yawing and creaking through a foghorn drone, the Sutherlands' version is a haunting lamentation, a salty reminder of what draws us to the swollen tide and what we leave behind. "Its roots are in the old hymns we sang as kids in the kirk," says Gavin Sutherland. "It's more of a spiritual metaphor than a literal reference." Stewart pitched 'Sailing' as a romantic anthem to distant lovers everywhere. "We were delighted to hear Rod's version," says Sutherland. "It was very different from ours; a much bigger production. It helped our careers a lot, bless him."

In 1976 the cover was used as the theme for *Sailor*, the popular BBC fly-on-the-boat documentary about the Ark Royal aircraft carrier. Re-released, it was punted back up the charts by a patriotic public stirred by the song's convection of elegiac defiance. It also, inevitably, became a soccer favourite. "Hearing it sung on the terraces for the first time was a real blast; even if it was 'We are Tott'nam'," says Sutherland. "And when the Navy started singing it, well that was just fine too, that's what songs are for. It's got a life of its own now, a proper folk song."

JACKIE WILSON SAID (I'M IN HEAVEN WHEN YOU SMILE)
DEXYS MIDNIGHT RUNNERS (1982)
Original by Van Morrison (1972)

As the poet Paul Durcan has noted, Van Morrison's songs are littered with the cadence of names. One of Morrison's greatest compositions, 'Jackie Wilson Said', was among the first pop songs to celebrate the emotional impact of one singer on another. Having already name-checked another cult soul hero on the hit 'Geno' (Washington), a dungareed Dexys Midnight Runners charted with a note-perfect copy of Morrison's original in 1982.

Wilson, known in his day as "Mr Excitement", scored a string of solo hits, beginning with 1957's 'Reet Petite (The Finest Girl You Ever Want to Meet)', and was a defining influence on the young Belfast boy. Van's tribute to the man Smokey Robinson called the most exciting entertainer he'd ever seen first appeared in 1972, opening the enigmatically-titled *Saint Dominic's Preview*. Van's album uniquely blended celtic folk, jazz, gospel with his own brand of metaphysical soul.

Mark Isham, the composer and trumpeter who played with Morrison during the Eighties, recalled Van's infatuation with the Detroit-born soul star. "He loves Jackie Wilson, who was pretty overtly sexual and rough around the edges. On the other hand, there's an aspect of that that drives Van crazy, because it isn't this higher-aesthetic thing."

Dexys' remake (on which Morrison declined an invitation to contribute) is also fondly remembered for a *Top of the Pops* performance, when the band inexplicably jigged before a billboard mugshot of darts player Jocky Wilson. As for Jackie himself, in 1961 he was shot and critically wounded by a demented fan – that was the official story, anyway: others say it was a jealous girlfriend who pulled the trigger. His career faltered through the Sixties and he suffered a heart attack on stage in Cherry Hill, New Jersey in 1975, striking his head as he fell. The resulting brain damage left him in a coma for more than eight years until his death a year or so after Dexys reminded us of a great song and an almost-forgotten legend.

THE BOOK OF LOVE
PETER GABRIEL (2004)
Original by the Magnetic Fields (1999)

Covers of Peter Gabriel songs have been rather hit and miss – Robert Wyatt's 'Biko' was suitably solemn, although Erasure's 4/4 disco version of 'Solsbury Hill' had most people running for the hills. On the few occasions Gabriel has tackled other people's songs, however, he generally adds to what is already there. He was introduced to the Magnetic Fields, fronted by Stephin Merritt, through a friend and was immediately taken with "the quirky way the band were interpreting songs". He was taken by one song in particular, from their sprawling 1999 album *69 Love Songs*, and pitched, unsuccessfully, to have them signed to his Real World label.

The track which caught Gabriel's ear was a tremulous guitar number, 'The Book of Love', which sounded a little like the Divine Comedy playing late period Nick Drake. Once heard it was difficult to forget and it was on his mind as he put finishing touches to his own 2002 album, *Up*. With time to spare during the dubbing of a string section to one of the tracks, he recorded a "simple string arrangement" for 'The Book of Love'. "We did it there and then," he said. Not fitting any Gabriel project at the time, the cover was sidelined onto the soundtrack for the 2004 movie *Shall We Dance?* "It was an effortless interpretation of a song where you really hear and feel the voice," Gabriel said. And it gave him an idea.

Gabriel began gathering material from like-minded artists, such as David Bowie, Bon Iver, Arcade Fire and Radiohead for a projected album of contemporary covers. *Scratch My Back*, arranged for just strings and voice, eventually appeared in 2010 and included a spruced up version of the Magnetic Fields' song. "There's a Slow Food movement," Gabriel said at the time. "I think I'm part of the Slow Music movement."

'The Book of Love' was issued as a digital download (Gabriel announced he would be releasing a two-song download on iTunes every full moon) and has been much used on TV – notably in *Scrubs* and *Desperate Housewives*. This has, naturally, benefited the otherwise low-profile Magnetic Fields. "Claudia from the Magnetic Fields tells me they are getting lots of requests for this particular version, with a string arrangement, for wedding ceremonies," says Gabriel. "My version of the song focuses on the humour, and his focuses on the pathos," Merritt told the *New York Times*. "Of course, if I could sing like him I wouldn't have to be a humourist."

TAINTED LOVE
SOFT CELL (1981)
Original by Gloria Jones (1965)

Northern soul mates Marc Almond and Dave Ball sweated it out to 'Tainted Love' in the Seventies. When their manager needed a debut single, the synth duo thought of Gloria. During the Sixties, ten years before she became the constant companion of a chubby Marc Bolan, Texas-born Gloria Jones was a jobbing soul singer with a powerful voice. Her original version of the Soft Cell hit is one of the great soul romps. Sparing us the conceit of 'I Will Survive' or simplistic rhetoric of 'Where Did Our Love Go', this is a defiant tale of good loving gone bad. Written by producer Ed Cobb and released on the Minit label, 'Tainted Love', acquired cult status with Northern Soul devotees.

Soft Cell's infectious electro-camp version was difficult to avoid in 1981. "We thought we were being twisted and ironic doing 'Tainted Love'," Almond told one American newspaper. "And the irony was that it became this huge pop hit. Suddenly, we found ourselves surrounded by screaming teenage girls and on the front of British pop magazines wearing silly party hats." Almond had mixed feelings about the song. "The minute 'Tainted Love' was a worldwide success, it was the beginning of the end."

Having unwittingly spawned a classic, Gloria Jones went on to produce hits for Marvin Gaye, Diana Ross and Gladys Knight and the Pips, hooking up with T. Rex in 1974. Bolan contributed guitar on her solo album *Vixen* and the couple had a son, Rolan. Their partnership ended in tragedy when Bolan was killed in a car accident in 1977, with Jones at the wheel.

Thanks to Soft Cell, her song has subsequently been covered by everyone from the Pussycat Dolls to Imelda May. In 2001 it was given a theatrical makeover by Marilyn Manson for the movie soundtrack of *Not Another Teen Movie*.

SORROW
DAVID BOWIE (1973)
Original by the McCoys (1965)

In November 1973 it was yesterday once more. Fifties throwback Alvin Stardust was all over the television and radiograms crackled to that month's new releases: the Who's backdated concept album *Quadrophenia*, Bryan Ferry's collection of oldies *These Foolish Things* and, most importantly, *Pin Ups*, David Bowie's chequered tribute to swinging London. Hot on the tiny heels of the ludicrous 'Laughing Gnome', *Pin Ups* was trailed by the wistfully nostalgic single 'Sorrow'.

Seven years earlier it had been a Top 10 hit for Liverpool duo the Merseys. Guitarist Tony Crane and bassist Billy Kinsley, formerly one half of the Merseybeats, were managed by the Who's business brains, Kit Lambert and Chris Stamp. In need of a hit, they recorded 'Sorrow' at the suggestion of the Who's road manager. It was penned by the production team of Bob Feldman, Jerry Goldstein and Richard Gottehrer, and only a few months earlier had surfaced as a B-side by Rick Derringer's mid-Sixties garage band the McCoys (better known for 'Hang On Sloopy').

Crane and Kinsley stripped the McCoys' version of its jingle-jangle whimsy, fleshed out the harmonies and battened down the beat. Tony Crane recalls the first sessions: "The original demo featured Jimmy Page on guitar, John Paul Jones on bass, Jack Bruce on string bass and Clem Cattini on drums," he says. "But the record company, Fontana, didn't like it." So the stellar session men were dropped and the recording re-arranged to include a brass section. The result was a top five hit in 1966. "We were delighted when Bowie decided to cover it. His favourite Merseybeat band: quite an honour!" says Crane. *Pin Ups*, however, was Bowie's first flawed album. "While *Pin Ups* may be a failure," crowed *Rolling Stone* magazine in 1973,

FURTHER LISTENING

Apart from *Pin Ups*, Bowie has peppered his back catalogue with some great cover versions. Here are six more from the Thin White Duke.

LET'S SPEND THE NIGHT TOGETHER (1973)

A frantic version of the Rolling Stones rebel classic, full of urgent teenage angst and juvenile delinquency and found on *Aladdin Sane*. The lyrics of the original were altered to "Let's spend some time together" when the Stones performed it on the *Ed Sullivan Show*.

TRY SOME, BUY SOME (2003)

Bowie's terrific cover of this overlooked George Harrison number graces the late-period album *Reality* and was recorded with genuine affection. It was originally written for Ronnie Spector, who released it as a single in 1971, and is also found on Harrison's 1973 own album *Living in the Material World*.

WILD IS THE WIND (1976)

First brought to Bowie's attention by Nina Simone, in a smoky, seductive version of the Johnny Mathis Fifties Western theme. Simone first recorded it on her *Live at Town Hall* album of 1957, but Bowie possibly first heard it as the title track to her 1966 album.

KNOCK ON WOOD (1974)

Already a hit twice over - for Eddie Floyd in 1967 and, the same year, Otis Redding and Carla Thomas (and again for Amii Stewart, in 1978) - Bowie's live cover of this soul stomper was lifted from his *Bowie Live* album and spun chartwards.

NITE FLIGHTS (1993)

Scott Walker's aeronautic song, originally the title track to the Walker Brothers 1978 swansong, has attracted a few artists, including the Fatima Mansions. Bowie has also covered Walker's interpretations of Jacque Brel's 'Amsterdam' and 'My Death'.

IT AIN'T EASY (1972)

Not by Ray Davies, as many originally thought, but Ron Davies, an early-Seventies also-ran singer-songwriter. It was covered by Long John Baldry and may have been suggested to Bowie for inclusion as the only cover on the *Ziggy Stardust* album by his guitarist Mick Ronson.

"it is also a collection of great songs, most of which are given a more than adequate, and always loving, treatment." With its long blonde hair and its eyes of blue, 'Sorrow' was Bowie's first cover to chart: it's charming, wistful and makes today seem rather sad.

KILLING ME SOFTLY WITH HIS SONG
ROBERTA FLACK (1973)
Original by Lori Lieberman (1971)

It's not often that airline music changes a career. Classy soulstress Roberta Flack first heard 'Killing Me Softly', performed by folk singer Lori Lieberman, on an in-flight headset in the early Seventies. So moved was Flack by Lieberman's intimate confessional, that on landing she set about tracking down its writers. "When I heard it, I freaked. I absolutely freaked," reported Flack. "When I got to New York, I went to the hotel and called Quincy Jones. I said, 'Tell me how to find the guys who wrote this song – Charles Fox and Norman Gimbel'."

'Killing Me Softly' began life as a poem. Lieberman took pen to paper after witnessing Don 'American Pie' McLean at the famous Troubadour Club on LA's Sunset Strip, and wrote 'Killing Me Softly With His Blues'. "I didn't know who he was," she later told journalists. "But from the moment he walked on stage, I was spellbound. I felt as if he knew me and his songs were about my life. I felt like he sang into my soul."

Gimbel and Fox reworked Lori's poem, gave it muscle and returned it to Lieberman, who recorded the track in 1971. Flack's version, produced by Joel Dorn, was released a couple of years later, topping the charts on both sides of the Atlantic. Flack, Gimbel and Fox all received Grammys. Lieberman, never officially credited as lyricist, was left to lick her wounds. The Fugees cut a version in 1996, which is more chilled out than flushed with fever, but was a huge hit nonetheless. Back in the Seventies, the municipal governors of Washington D.C., where Flack had studied, were so impressed with their alumna's achievements, she was presented with the keys to the city and April 22 was declared Roberta Flack Day.

I SHOT THE SHERIFF
ERIC CLAPTON (1974)
Original by the Wailers (1973)

Holed up in a white stucco mansion under the swaying palms on Miami's Ocean Boulevard, Eric Clapton and his team were piecing together the album that would be Slowhand's great comeback from a prolonged heroin-induced hiatus. Blues guitarist George Terry rolled up with keen grin and a Bob Marley and the Wailers record under his arm. In 1974 reggae was hardly taken seriously by the musical establishment, so when Terry spun *Burnin'*, Clapton was unsure which way to jump. "It took me a while to get into it, to tell you the truth," said Eric later in interview. "To break my inherent musical tightness down into this real loose thing was very, very difficult for me to assimilate." Clapton eventually loosened up. "I told Eric 'give the rhythm some time'," recalled Terry. "The feel was so different from the blues changes that are his love and his roots. But I could see he was getting into the beat, the soul, and Marley's great lyrics."

The band spent the next day in the studio riffing through Eric's favourite track, the audacious 'I Shot the Sheriff'. It's a bold declaration of innocence, guilt and smoking guns. "We all came under the spell of the song," recalled Terry, "but I was still a little surprised when Eric turned to me and said, 'Let's cut it!'." 'Sheriff' was a Top 10 for Clapton and the accompanying album, *461 Ocean Boulevard*, hailed as classic soft-rock. The single not only helped revive a troubled career, it also showcased Marley's prodigious songwriting talents and made reggae respectable for a rock audience.

Did the shoot-out with Sheriff John Brown and his deputy actually happen? When asked about the song's origins, Marley was cagey. "I want to say 'I shot the police' but the government would have made a fuss, so I said 'I shot the sheriff'." Clapton reckoned he got little more out of him. "He wouldn't really commit himself. He said that some parts of it were true, but he wasn't going to say which parts."

ALWAYS ON MY MIND
PET SHOP BOYS (1987)
Original by Brenda Lee (1972)

In 1987, the Pet Shop Boys were invited to contribute to a show commemorating the tenth anniversary of Elvis Presley's death. "We were approached by Central TV to be on a programme called *Love Me Tender*," recalled Neil Tennant. "And for some reason we agreed to do it." The Boys were sent a cache of old Elvis cassettes to wade through. Not being particular fans, they settled on the first song on the first tape they listened to: 'Always on my Mind'.

Long-time Elvis sideman Red West had brought 'Always on my Mind' to Presley's recording sessions at the RCA Hollywood Studios in March 1972. It was penned by Wayne Thompson, Mark James and Johnny Christopher, and had just been recorded by Brenda Lee. Presley cut his version, along with West's own offering, 'Separate Ways', for seven-inch release. These two tear-stained ballads flutter like pages from Presley's own diary. Only days earlier he and Priscilla had parted company, following Elvis's refusal to allow his wife to accompany him on tour and Priscilla's subsequent affair with a karate instructor. "Maybe I didn't treat you quite as good as I should have", mourns the self-reproaching opener. "What are you guys trying to do to me?" Elvis reportedly barked when he read the lyrics in the studio. He liked the song though and eventually made it gold, before filing for divorce and hitting the road again.

The Pet Shop Boys chose it because it came from, as they put it, his "bloated Vegas" period. "Chris came up with the brass riff, and I put a different chord in at the end of the chorus, a B flat, which made it more disco-sounding," said Tennant. Their austere version, with its digital pulse and matter-of-fact vocal, cleverly transforms lachrymose melodrama into callous apathy. Released as a single at the end of the year, it was a bigger hit than the original and a not very cheerful Christmas Number One in the UK.

DELILAH
ALEX HARVEY (1975)
Original by Tom Jones (1968)

As a 20-year-old in the mid Fifties, Alex Harvey was briefly hailed as the "Scottish Tommy Steele". Skillfully avoiding all that such an accolade might have promised, the Gorbals-born singer instead hooked up with rocker Gene Vincent, fronted various blues combos and served a stint as guitarist in the musical *Hair*, before forming the Sensational Alex Harvey Band in 1972. SAHB were an ardent blend of comic-book ham-glam, Glaswegian vaudeville and enough hard-nosed riffs to give you a headache till next Thursday. Their first chart success was a mettlesome version of the song that made Tom Jones a household name.

'Delilah', a violent *crime passionel* from the charmed pens of songwriters Les Reed and Barry Mason, was inspired by a holiday romance. Mason was a spotty teenager when he met a girl called Delia in Blackpool. "I fell in love with her when I was 15 and it was really a heavy affair of the heart," he revealed to the BBC in 2001. Delia, however, resisted the lad's advances. "She said 'no, I have a boyfriend' and that was my first broken heart." Mason was still prickled by the experience years later as he composed the famous ballad of revenge for P.J. Proby (whose version remained unreleased until 2008, after Proby dismissed it as a German *bierkeller* song). It was down to Tom Jones to make it famous. "Delia really did not fit into the song and then we thought of Delilah... a classic femme fatale in history." Jones was delighted. "When I recorded 'Delilah', I knew it was different, but I didn't know if it was commercial enough to be a hit." The public did, though, and sent it to the top of the pops in February 1968.

Seven years on, SAHB's treatment, all deadpan theatrics, earsplitting guitar and comedy organ hooks, is a long way from

Jones' smouldering performance. There's cold desperation in Harvey's voice, the knife plunging with each rhetorical "Why?" It, too, was a big hit, but the band felt misunderstood. "Because Alex comes from a rough area of Glasgow, I think they reckon us to be uncouth, violent sex maniacs," bassist Chris Glenn told *Sounds* in 1975. "We're all right, really."

SHE'S NOT THERE
SANTANA (1977)
Original by the Zombies (1964)

Written by the Zombies' 19-year-old keyboard player, Rod Argent, 'She's Not There' was the first Top 20 hit to feature the electric piano as lead instrument. "It was only the second song I had written," says Argent. "We entered a local beat competition in St Albans and won a recording deal. The debut single was going to be a version of 'Summertime' but Ken Jones at Decca said 'you ought to write something for the session'." Argent began casting around for ideas. "I'd been listening to a lot of jazz and blues," he recalls. "I played a track by John Lee Hooker that began with the line 'No one told me.' Lyrically, that was the starting point." Musically, Argent was eager to emulate his jazz heroes and experimented with tempo, phrasing and staggered meter.

The result was as complex as any contemporary Beatles recording. It got the thumbs-up from George Harrison on TV's *Juke Box Jury*, which helped it into the charts in 1964, and became a huge influence on many musicians. "Years later the jazz guitarist Pat Metheny told me it was what inspired him to move in a rock direction," says Argent. Metheny wasn't alone in his admiration. Carlos Santana's Latin-fusion take on the British beat classic was a surprise hit for the guitarist in 1977. The song tiptoes in on Mexican wave of marimbas, bongos and timbales. Carlos curves his Gibson around the percussion, dashing about like Speedy Gonzalez and trading riffs with the rhythm section. It kicks like jalapeno pepper jelly and effectively revived the guitarist's career in the late Seventies. "I absolutely loved his version," praised Argent, delighted that Santana took his song south of the border. "Although it's obviously not a Latin composition, the original does have Latin elements in it."

MADNESS
MADNESS (1979)
Original by Prince Buster (1963)

Cecil Bustamante Campbell, aka Prince Buster, is one of the founders of modern dance music. Born on Kingston's Orange Street – reggae's main drag – in 1938, Buster was a crucial figure in the development of ska, an exciting postwar blend of American R&B, calypso and Jamaican "mento" boogie. By the late Fifties, he was rocking and grooving Kingston's dance halls with a revolutionary twin-deck sound system, 'Voice of the People'. "The whole town is crazy beca' Prince Buster build a sound," he commented.

Having made his name as a DJ, in 1961 Buster signed to London's Blue Beat records and began commercially recording. 'Madness' first appeared on the 1963 album *I Feel The Spirit* and was released as a single. It's a delirious mishmash of piano, guitar and horns, all clinging white-knuckle to the offbeat. "Madness, madness, I call it gladness", declares Buster, with little elaboration. In Britain the Mods loved the way it sizzles like a snapper-fish and fits like a porkpie hat.

By the late Sixties, a new generation of inner-city white kids was rocking steady at the youth club disco. "We really liked the music of Prince Buster," recalled Suggs. "When we grew up, because of the influx of people from Jamaica, you would hear the music of Desmond Dekker, you would hear the Maytals, they'd be on the pop radio. So we mixed all that music up together when we formed the band." Madness was among the first of the ska revival acts signed to the 2-Tone label in 1979. Their debut release was a version of the song that gave them their name. Backed with their own homage to Buster, 'The Prince', it was an instant hit. The nutty boys were never shy to acknowledge their debt to the King of Ska, scoring the following year with Buster's party-favourite instrumental 'One Step Beyond'.

ELOISE
THE DAMNED (1986)
Original by Barry Ryan (1968)

By 1986 most punk bands had hung up the bondage pants. With just two founder members still in the saddle, the Damned – once described by Johnny Rotten as "a very dirty version of the Bay City Rollers" – were the last of the Mohicans, basking in their own Indian summer. Their biggest success was an unlikely cover of a melodramatic song which had first gushed up the charts like a burst faucet in 1968.

Groomed for stardom and pitched as a sort of British Everlys, Yorkshire twins Paul and Barry Ryan were regular callers on the Top 20 before Paul's nerves got the better of him and he slipped into the shadows to concentrate on songwriting. 'Eloise', penned for his brother, was Paul's *magnum opus*. Densely orchestrated in the mould of Scott Walker's bon vivant 'Jackie' and echoing Richard Harris's arrangement of 'MacArthur Park', this tale of unrequited love was one of the first singles to be promoted with a video and was an immediate smash, selling three million copies. It was the one and only Top 10 hit for Barry Ryan, who went on to work as an acclaimed photographer. Paul Ryan died in 1992.

Fronted by vocalist and former gravedigger Dave Vanian, the Damned's version pounds away like fists on a coffin lid. "One of the things I like most about it is all the different meanings you can get from the lyric," drummer and ex-toilet-cleaner Rat Scabies reported to one interviewer. "My interpretation of the lyrics is of a schizophrenic drag artist." According to Scabies, though, Ryan divulged to him the true inspiration for the song. "It was actually written about a stripper. So Barry was telling us."

ROLL OVER BEETHOVEN
ELECTRIC LIGHT ORCHESTRA (1972)
Original by Chuck Berry (1956)

In the late Fifties St. Louis-born Chuck Berry was a player of extraordinary influence and innovation. He is also author of a bunch of brash, lyrical ditties that defined the teenage experience for a generation to come. 'Roll Over Beethoven' was his fourth single on Chess Records, released in 1956. Chuck wraps his big-boned hands around his famous red Gibson and deals a three-chord trick that perfectly articulates the excitement and vitality of this new music. This was the first song *about* rock 'n' roll. It was a live favourite in the Sixties and Seventies, with everyone from the Beatles to Uriah Heap.

The Electric Light Orchestra's deft, eight-minute arrangement of Berry's classic, with its layered strings, scorching guitar and tongue-in-cheek quotes from Beethoven's Fifth, raised their prog-pop profile. "We're not into experimental classical stuff, nothing discordant. I just love the melodies of the old composers," reckoned Jeff Lynne. The full-length version featured on the band's second album, the overblown *ELO 2*. Trimmed down to a more manageable four minutes, it was earmarked for release on 45 in January 1973, by which time it was already a popular encore number. The band's drummer, Bev Bevan, called it "perhaps the most important single we ever made".

In 2000 Berry's pianist and sideman, Johnnie Johnson, filed a lawsuit against his former boss, claiming that he co-wrote 'Roll Over Beethoven' (and several other Berry hits) and where were his royalties? Some acrimonious mud-slinging ensued before a judge through the case out of court, ruling that too many years had elapsed since the disputed songs were written. In truth Berry probably converted one of Johnson's boogie piano riffs to guitar and added the lyrics, but the sound is all his own. As the old ELO gag goes: never play second fiddle; it'll only end in violins.

Covered almost as much as the Beatles, Dylan's position as one of the twentieth century's most important songwriters was established early in his career. What is extraordinary is how many of his songs have been so definitively recorded by others. Adele's cover of "Make You Feel My Love" makes way for six more barbs from the Bard.

KNOCKIN' ON HEAVEN'S DOOR
GUNS N' ROSES (1992)
Slash and co began including this Dylan strum-along in live sets in the late Eighties. They recorded a studio version first for a movie soundtrack and then again for the album *Use Your Illusion II* in 1992.

I THREW IT ALL AWAY
ELVIS COSTELLO (1995)
Also covered by Scott Walker, this *Nashville Skyline* track, with its plunging bassline, was borrowed by Costello for his 1995 covers collection *Kojak Variety*, a curious set actually recorded some years earlier.

IF NOT FOR YOU
GEORGE HARRISON (1970)
Dylan's friend Harrison included this *New Morning* track on his post-Beatles triple set All Things Must Pass. Shortly afterwards

A HARD RAIN'S A-GONNA FALL
BRYAN FERRY (1973)
Original by Bob Dylan (1963)

Covered by many – from Leon Russell to Edie Brickell – 'A Hard Rain's A-Gonna Fall' remains one of Bob Dylan's least proselytising and persistently relevant protest songs and as chill a track as any from the politically troubled early Sixties. Dylan's second album – *Freewheelin' Bob Dylan* – was released on the eve of the young folk singer's 22nd birthday, in 1963.

it was an easy listening hit for Olivia Newton-John and has also been covered by Rod Stewart and Glen Campbell.

ALL ALONG THE WATCHTOWER
JIMI HENDRIX (1967)

Was Hendrix inspired to record this after catching the psychedelic jazzer Alan Bown perform his version in a London club? Bown took his version to the studio before Hendrix, although it was released long afterwards. Either way, Hendrix made it firmly his own.

MR TAMBOURINE MAN
THE BYRDS (1965)

The track that helped launch American folk rock into the mainstream. This *Bringing it all Back Home* track was first heard by the Byrds on acetate. When Dylan heard their jangly cover he exclaimed enthusiastically, "Wow, you can dance to that!"

THE MIGHTY QUINN
MANFRED MANN (1968)

Like 'This Wheel's on Fire', this was originally recorded by Dylan during his sojourn at Big Pink in 1967, as part of the "Basement Tapes" sessions, and much bootlegged. It wasn't officially released by Dylan for another three years, meanwhile becoming a huge UK hit for South African exile Manfred Mann.

'A Hard Rain's A-Gonna Fall' is "a desperate kind of song", says its composer on the liner notes to the original album sleeve. Dylan wrote it during the Cuban missile crisis of the previous year, while the world hung on a thread. "Every line in it is actually the start of a whole song," he told journalist Nat Hentoff, with typical self-agrandisement. "But when I wrote it, I thought I wouldn't have enough time alive to write all those songs so I put all I could into this one." Dylan's lines jostle and alliterate in a reportage of war that is rarely so eloquent and so appalling.

A decade on, in an altogether more decadent time than that

bleak fortnight in October 1962, Bryan Ferry was busy reinventing himself and piecing together his first solo album – *These Foolish Things* – comprising a crop of covers of Smokey Robinson, Goffin and King, the Rolling Stones and Leiber and Stoller, amongst others. The opener was a tremulous and inventive rendition of 'A Hard Rain' which, as a seven-inch, trailed the album's release in 1973. "I think it's a beautiful song, although I can't be bothered with all that Cuba crisis stuff," reported Ferry to the *NME*. "I like the images... To me a cover is just changing the vocal performance. I like to redesign a song."

Ferry's treatment was indeed a radical departure from Dylan's original. "Virtually anything you did would have been different because all he did was guitar and voice and mouth organ," Ferry said in interview. "So I did it over the top, real kind of pounding piano and everything, sound effects and so on. It was really good. I enjoyed that."

I FOUGHT THE LAW
THE CLASH (1979)
Original by the Crickets (1959)

Some songs are just born bad. 'I Fought the Law' was a hit twice over for the Clash. First on the *Cost of Living* EP – wedged ignobly between the band's second and third albums and released the day Margaret Thatcher came to power – and again in 1988. It was penned by Sonny Curtis of the Crickets and originally intended as a Buddy Holly single, but recording never took place and it was left to his former backing band to cut the song posthumously after Holly's death in 1959, with guitarist Henry Earl Sinks taking lead vocals. The song wasn't a hit, but it didn't go un-noticed.

In 1964, fellow Texan and Holly soundalike Bobby Fuller pulled up at his El Paso studio, wiped an oily rag round the mike and dropped the clutch on one of the great garage-band anthems. The Bobby Fuller Four version of 'I Fought the Law' is a paradigmatic tale of crime and punishment. This time the law won and our ne'er-do-well got caught. Now he's breaking rocks under the Texas sun: it hurts and he's missing his baby.

Fuller's guitar phrasing and smacked tambourine owes much to the Holly sound. It charted a couple of years later and on the back of its success the Four were tipped for stardom, but it was not to be. A few weeks later, Fuller's body was discovered stretched across the front seat of his mother's '62 Oldsmobile, beaten, bruised and with a stomach full of gasoline. Mystery surrounds his death: implausibly the coroner settled on suicide; others have speculated murder, possibly by the mob.

Despite its association with two rock deaths, 'I Fought the Law' has been a popular cover and like 'Louie Louie' is a perfect example of American punk of the mid Sixties. Perfect, too, for the latter day residents of garageland UK. Recorded at

Stoke Newington's Wessex Studios in the winter of 1978/79, the Clash deliver with machine-gun fire, It's a cracking riff and the band give it their all. Buddy would have loved it.

STAND BY ME
JOHN LENNON (1975)
Original by Ben E. King (1961)

John Lennon resumed work on his parboiled collection of rock 'n' roll oldies in October 1974, a year after producer Phil Spector had made off with the master tapes and the ill-fated project shook, rattled and rolled into contractual confusion. "It started in '73 with Phil and fell apart," said Lennon. "I ended up as part of mad, drunk scenes in Los Angeles and I finally finished it off on me own. I can't begin to say, it's just barmy, there's a jinx on that album." This Ben E. King evergreen helped complete the troubled back-to-basics set.

The title, as the composer and former Drifters lead tenor recalled, was inspired by an old gospel number from Sam Cooke and the Soul Stirrers, 'Stand By Me, Father': "I snuck that 'stand' bit out and started writing it." In 1961 King took it to his producers. "I was doing a session with Jerry Leiber and Mike Stoller. We finished the recording and they said, 'look, we've got a few seconds left, have you got any songs?' I showed them 'Stand By Me'." Leiber and Stoller loved it, worked up a string arrangement and eventually assumed co-writing credits.

An early cover is the 1963 one by Cassius Clay, soon to become Muhammad Ali. The original was an early favourite of the Beatles, in particular Lennon. In 1974 he demoed it during his stint as collaborator on Harry Nilsson's own retro compilation, *Pussy Cats*. The historic line-up included Lennon, Nilsson, Stevie Wonder and, on drums, Paul McCartney, who just happened to be in town. In their last ever studio pairing the two ex-Beatles took a few casual shots at 'Stand By Me' and half a dozen other covers – none destined for official release – sharing vocals and joking and bickering as the mood caught them.

The version that made it onto Lennon's *Rock 'n' roll*, and into the Top Twenty, was cut at Roy Cicala's Record Plant East studios in Manhattan. Backed by a roster of A-list session men, Lennon delivers a passionate rendition. One take was caught on camera for the BBC's *Old Grey Whistle Test*, an appearance for which he allegedly demanded a characteristically Lennonesque fee – eight boxes of chocolate Bath Oliver biscuits.

GET DOWN AND GET WITH IT
SLADE (1971)
Original by Bobby Marchan (1964)

Bobby Marchan was fascinated by the female impersonators he saw working the southern States' "chitlin' circuit" of black nightclubs during the early Fifties. Born Oscar James Gibson in Youngstown, Ohio in 1930, Marchan formed the Powder Box Revue in 1953, a drag act who soon came, not unsurprisingly, to the attention of Little Richard, the original Georgia Peach. Around discussions over make-up and music, Richard and Marchan formed a natural bond. While Richard shook his tutti-frutti up the charts, Marchan label-hopped his way through the Fifties and into the Sixties, releasing discs for Dot and Aladdin, Ace and Stax.

A year or so after it was first issued on the tiny Dial imprint, Richard cut his own version of Marchan's ever so slightly camp but funky rabble-rouser. 'Get Down With it', as it was originally titled, was the perfect finger-snapping, testifying cover. Richard whoops and hollers his way through a piano-crunching take on the song, sweeping aside the original in a glorious cloud of powder puff. By the late Sixties, the song had become a show-closer for Slade, a struggling bunch of over-stylised boot boys from Wolverhampton. "It was a very basic twelve-bar blues track," wrote Noddy Holder in his autobiography, *Who's Crazee Now*, "but it had something magical about it." Audiences indeed went crazee for the revamped soul stomper. "It was a storming song to finish with and it somehow summed up what Slade were all about," Holder recalled.

'Get Down and Get With it' was the sound upon which Slade had built a boisterous stage reputation. Aiming to capture the live excitement on vinyl, manager Chas Chandler pitched for their Little Richard cover as a single. Recorded in the raw at Olympic studio, in front of an imaginary audience, the band nailed it in one take. But it still lacked something. "Because of technical constraints, the song was nowhere near as heavy as it was at our gigs," said Holder. Chandler set up microphones on the stairs outside the studio and taped the band clapping and stamping, their combined pounding echoing up the stairwell. After several overdubs, it was done. Also included on their classic concert album, *Slade Alive!*, 'Get Down and Get With it' was the first of Slade's run of rowdy floor fillers, prompting the band to swap their ill-fitting skinhead image for heels and glitter. Little Richard must surely have approved.

WALK AWAY RENEE
THE FOUR TOPS (1968)
Original by the Left Banke (1966)

Tamla Motown's hitmaking team of Holland, Dozier and Holland provided the Four Tops with an impressive run of chart entries in the mid Sixties. When they quit the corporation in 1967 to set up the rival Invictus label, they left Detroit's premier vocal quartet singing the same old song. It was time for Motown to shop around. Label boss Berry Gordy looked to white pop to complete the Tops' album *Reach Out*, selecting songs by Tim Hardin, the Monkees and this minor hit by a classically-influenced, hirsute foursome called the Left Banke.

The harmonic 'Walk Away Renee' was written by the Left Banke's 16-year-old keyboard player, Michael Brown, real name Mike Lookofsky, and his writing partners Tony Sansone and Bob Calilli. When a bandmate brought along his platinum blonde girlfriend, Renee Fladen, to their New York recording studio, Brown's metronome skipped a beat. The song he wrote for her perfectly expresses his unrequited love. To emphasise the lost-love theme Sansone contributed lines about one-way streets and empty sidewalks, but it's Brown's heart-wrenching chorus that you remember: "Just walk away Renee / You won't see me follow you back home."

"It's the ultimate love song," Brown told *Rolling Stone* magazine. "It's about loving someone enough to set them free." During recording, Brown's muse gazed down from the control room as he tracked his harpsichord part. "My hands were shaking when I tried to play," he recalled. "There was no way I could do it with her around, so I came back and did it later."

The original version of 'Renee', a US hit in 1966, tinkles like a baroque chandelier caught in the melodic breeze of mid-Sixties American pop. It's the muscular voice of the Four Tops' lead singer Levi Stubbs and the lush Motown production that transforms this frilly-shirted curio into one of the most memorable records of the period, a Top Five hit in the UK, and a regular feature of "best songs ever" charts. "There's a certain purity to [the song]," Brown later said. "And its purity comes from the idea that a dream lives, even if it's just as a fantasy."

DENIS
BLONDIE (1978)
Original by Randy and the Rainbows (1963)

'Denis' was Blondie's chart debut, a sassy slice of pop-punk that climaxed at Number Two in March 1978. Coming from the pen of songwriter Neil Levenson, it began life 15 years earlier as 'Denise' and was a Stateside hit for New York's Randy and the Rainbows.

Vinny Carella of the Rainbows takes up the story: "Neil wrote a song called 'Pretty Girl'. After meeting a girl at the beach named Denise LeFrak, he changed the song title to her name." Looking for a new group to trial his song, Levenson met a vocal quintet from Queens called the Encores. Impressed with the harmonic sixteen-year-olds, he introduced his discovery to fellow doo-woppers the Tokens, who renamed them Randy and the Rainbows and produced the group's recording of 'Denise'. It hit the charts with a bullet in the summer of 1963 and launched the teenagers on a coast-to-coast tour, performing alongside the likes of Stevie Wonder and the Beach Boys. Things went a bit quiet for the Rainbows after that, but in 2001 they returned with a new album, *Play Ball*, featuring a newly-recorded club mix of 'Denise'.

So how did the Rainbows feel when Blondie put the power-pop into doo-wop? "Neil called to tell me he got word from his publisher that a punk rock group would be covering 'Denise'," recalls Carella. "Initially, he wasn't happy. I remember him saying 'they ruined my song'." Carella thought it was great and suggested to Levenson that maybe he'd get a hit with it all over again. "[Blondie's guitarist] Chris Stein told me they were looking for something to get them going. They had a K-Tel album with 'Denise' on it, so they reworked it in their genre and it jump started their career."

Blondie fell apart in the early Eighties, but in 1999 their muse made an unexpected reappearance, as Stein explained. "I was going to sell a couple of my gold records. I called up a rock-and-roll collector who turned out to be the husband of Jackie LeFrak. And her sister was the girl 'Denise' was written about." Stein took it as a good omen.

LIGHT MY FIRE
JOSE FELICIANO (1968)
Original by the Doors (1967)

This 1967 Doors stalwart has been set ablaze by numerous artists. The yardstick by which all covers of 'Light My Fire' are measured, though, is the version by Latin star Jose Feliciano. This 1968 recording was prompted by Feliciano's A&R man, Rick Jarrard, who played Jose the Doors' track, suggesting he slow it down and inject it with a little soul, aided by strings, bass, conga drums and a jazz flute. It was an overnight hit and shifted a million.

The song was written by the Doors' guitarist Robby Krieger, who presented his demo to Jim Morrison and the band as they pieced together their debut album. "Jim was really great about doing my songs. I tried to write about universal themes like he did," Krieger has said. "I did it about fire, because fire was one of the four elements. I also wrote quite a few water songs."

In his autobiography, also entitled *Light My Fire*, the Doors' keyboard player Ray Manzarek explains how they worked on Krieger's prototype. "John [Densmore, drummer] came up with a very cool Latino beat for the verse and the four-on-the-floor hard-rock beat for the chorus. Worked like a mother." Morrison contributed a verse and Manzarek topped it all off with a rococo organ riff: "Run some back filigrees over the top in a kind of turning-in-on-itself Fibonacci spiral – like a nautilus shell – and you've got it."

Krieger's playing is just as serpentine: "The chords are based on [John] Coltrane's version of 'My Favorite Things'. He just solos over A minor and B minor, which is exactly what we did." It was a perfect vehicle for Jim Morrison's audacious sexuality and provided the Doors with the breakthrough they needed. "Everything was there," said Manzarek. "The song was great. The parts were great. The groove was in the pocket."

41

FURTHER LISTENING

Of course, there are just a few more Beatles covers than there are holes in Blackburn, Lancashire. Here are six Fab interpretations from the last six decades.

SGT PEPPER'S LONELY HEART'S CLUB BAND
JIMI HENDRIX (1967)

Hendrix was the first major artist to cover anything from the Beatles' eighth album, performing his version of the title track at London's Saville Theatre just three days after its release. He reprised his version at the Isle of Wight festival in 1970, found on the album *Hendrix in the West*.

GOT TO GET YOU INTO MY LIFE
EARTH, WIND AND FIRE (1978)

The Grammy-award winning cover from the disastrous movie *Sgt Pepper's Lonely Heart's Club Band*. All trumpet stabs, scat singing and groovy guitar, it was a huge chart hit at a time when the Fabs legacy was wilting in the face of punk and disco.

HELTER SKELTER
U2 (1988)

"This is the song Charles Manson stole from the Beatles. We're stealing it back," Bono told his audience on the live version of the *White Album* song and proto-metal shrieker, found on *Rattle and Hum*.

I AM THE WALRUS
OASIS (1994)

From flip side to flip side. Originally the reverse of 1967's 'Hello, Goodbye', the Oasis note-copy take on Lennon's famous nonsense song was the B-side to their 'Cigarettes and Alcohol'.

SHE SAID, SHE SAID
THE BLACK KEYS (2002)

Wonderfully tight slab of grunge recorded in a basement on an eight-track tape recorder for the two-man band's debut album. One of *Revolver*'s best songs done the way Lennon would have appreciated it.

GOLDEN SLUMBERS/THE END
k.d. lang (2010)

The Fabs' final vinyl offering given a gentle jazz-lounge makeover by Canada's first lady of torch and twang for the album *Recollection*.

Robby Krieger has claimed he's never heard the song covered properly. The 2002 hit version by Will Young lacks combustible material of any kind, smouldering more like a Home Counties barbecue than a nocturnal seduction in the Mojave desert. The song has come a long way from Fibonacci and John Coltrane.

DEAR PRUDENCE
SIOUXSIE AND THE BANSHEES (1983)
Original by the Beatles (1968)

Deprived of electricity at the Maharishi Mahesh Yogi's transcendental meditation retreat at Rishikesh, John, Paul and George finger-picked their way through a suitcase of songs on acoustic guitars. The inspiration for this delicate Lennon number was their fellow traveller Prudence Farrow, sister of Mia, who was something of a recluse at the Himalayan hideout. "Prudence meditated and hibernated," remembered Ringo. "We saw her twice in two weeks. Everyone would be banging on the door: 'Are you still alive?'." Lennon figured music would coax her from her chalet: "All the people around her were worried about the girl because she was going insane. So we sang to her."

The competition at the Maharishi's ashram was who was going to "get cosmic" first. "She'd been locked in for three weeks and wouldn't come out, trying to reach God quicker than anybody else," said Lennon. Back in London, at the end of a steamy August Bank Holiday, the group (sans Ringo) entered Trident Studios to record and mix 'Dear Prudence'. Carefully pieced together track by track, with Lennon's vocals dubbed twice over, it shimmers in the summer haze.

The song made second billing on the hegemonic double set *The Beatles*, wafting in on the jetstream of 'Back in the USSR'. The album was a primary influence on the Banshees. "The Beatles got slated for it when it was released, it was unbelievable, but there's just something about that record," said Siouxsie. "One of the main reasons we chose ['Dear Prudence'] was that John Lennon's version sounds a bit unfinished," concurred bassist Steve Severin. "We recorded it in Sweden, and the idea came from touring round Scandinavia, listening to the Beatles." On their version, included on the band's covers album *Through the Looking Glass*, Siouxsie is a siren bewitched, luring us through the swirling mist and urging us to come out and play. In October 1983, as human chains of CND demonstrators encircled RAF Greenham Common and across the country industrial unrest loomed, 'Dear Prudence' was a call from Britain's dark side – more like a winter of discontent than an Indian summer. It was Siouxsie's biggest hit, kept off the top spot, much to the band's annoyance, by the feckless 'Karma Chameleon'.

I GO TO SLEEP
THE PRETENDERS (1982)
Original by the Kinks (1965)

As the Kinks prepared for a major US tour in May 1965, Ray Davies's wife Rasa was in hospital awaiting delivery of their baby. Davies paced the lino at home and dusted the piano for distraction. The next day Rasa gave birth to their daughter and Davies had written a lullaby for her: 'I Go To Sleep'. Within days the band took off for America. "Before the tour I had gone to a small studio in Denmark Street and made a very rough demo of the song, which I had sent to Peggy Lee," Davies recalled. On the sleeve of the first Kinks album, he cites the veteran jazz singer as one of his favourite performers.

Lee liked what she heard and returned the compliment. Backed by a studio orchestra under the direction of stalwart conductor Sid Feller, she cut 'I Go To Sleep' for her 1965 album, *Then Was Then – Now Is Now!* Despite the great lady's vocal talents, it's a somewhat perfunctory attempt; as clipped and brusque as a reprimand. It was, nevertheless, a feather in the cap for Ray. 'I Go To Sleep' might have snoozed off the radar had it not been for Sonny and Cher who, probably thanks to Davies' manager, came by the song and put it on their first album. It subsequently took a mid-Sixties beat makeover from outfits such as the Truth and the Applejacks, but with little chart success.

The Pretenders' 1982 reading, recorded whilst Chrissie Hynde and Ray Davies were mixing music and pleasure, is, by contrast, terrific. The plaintive horn riff and distant guitar get right to the heart of the song and make it the perfect two-way family favourite. Hynde claimed she heard neither Peggy Lee's original nor Cher's copy before recording her version. "The song publishers for about the first three Kinks albums sent me a cassette of a demo made by Ray Davies in 1965, with him playing piano. The Kinks never recorded it," Hynde said in interview. "In my estimation it's a perfect song and I was delighted to have access to it. I was just hoping they wouldn't be offended." And did Ray approve? "I don't know. He's never actually said."

THIS FLIGHT TONIGHT
NAZARETH (1973)
Original by Joni Mitchell (1971)

Joni Mitchell's confessional *Blue*, released in 1971, was a hot and bothered affair. Twinkling in the album's taillights is 'This Flight Tonight'. Behind Mitchell's stripped-down jazz inflexion and lonesome guitar, a pedal steel, courtesy of Sneaky Pete Kleinow, briefly meows in the sadness. Otherwise it's just us and Joni, and a vignette of stars burning up over the Las Vegas sands.

Dunfermline hard-rockers Nazareth loved *Blue*. Their gat-toothed vocalist Dan McCafferty had hair like a kitchen scourer and a voice to match. As their sophomore hit went, they were bad, bad boys. Among the tracks on their 1973 album, *Loud 'N' Proud*, produced by former Deep Purple bassist Roger Glover, is a rumbling version of 'This Flight'. "We used to listen to Joni as we were travelling round in the van," recalls Nazareth's bass player Pete Agnew. "'This Flight Tonight' was a big favourite." They were quick to see the song's potential to rock, took it into the studio and turned it on its head. "We only wanted to do cover versions on the basis that if you can change it enough, it becomes yours. If you can't change it, don't do it," Agnew says. Their bass-heavy version leaves Joni's crazy bird taxiing on the runway.

Mitchell was impressed with the makeover: "When she was recording at A&M, we were just starting an American tour," explains Agnew. "We all happened to be in the studio the day the single was released, so we were introduced to her and told her what we had done." Mitchell was amazed: "She said, 'What, with a rock band?'" Joni paid the Scottish band the greatest compliment after 'This Flight Tonight' became a worldwide hit for them, touching down at Number 11 in the UK. "She was playing a gig in London and told the audience: 'I'd like to open with a Nazareth song'!" remembers Agnew.

FURTHER LISTENING

Don't forget Winona! From Boulder to Birmingham, Chicago to LA, songs about US towns and cities have been particularly popular as cover versions. Stick a pin on six more stopovers from pop's glove-box gazetteer:

MEMPHIS TENNESSEE
Silicon Teens (1979)

Long distance information... Everyone it seems has had a crack at this 1963 Chuck Berry paean to long-distance love. Mute Records' Daniel Miller invented a whole imaginary band (line up: Darryl, Jacki, Paul and Diane) for his one-man synth-pop cover.

DETROIT CITY
Tom Jones (1967)

In 1963, country star Billy Grammer was the first to record this number about 'making cars in Motor City' and dreaming of cotton fields back home. It was made famous by the twangtastic Bobby Bare before providing Tom Jones with a worthy international follow up to his cover of Porter Wagoner's "Green Green Grass of Home".

GET OUT OF DENVER
Dave Edmunds (1977)

Also belted out by Eddie and the Hot Rods, this word-heavy cover of a long-lost Bob Seger single from '74 kicks off Dave Edmunds' splendid post-pub rock solo album *Get It* (which also features Nick Lowe). It kept Denver, Colorado on the musical map and Edmunds in the charts.

BY THE TIME I GET TO PHOENIX
GLEN CAMPBELL (1969)
Original by Johnny Rivers (1966)

'Gentle on my Mind' made Glen Campbell a star in 1967. Whilst casting around for a follow-up, the country-pop singer picked up a Johnny Rivers album, *Changes*, released the previous year. Campbell's eye was drawn to a title that fascinated him: 'By the Time I Get to Phoenix'. Written by a

WHAT'S MADE MILWAUKEE FAMOUS (HAS MADE A LOSER OUT OF ME)
Rod Stewart (1972)

It was beer that made the industrial port of Milwaukee, in southeast Wisconsin, famous. And it was Jerry Lee Lewis who, in 1968, first took this Glenn Sutton-penned song to the studio. The curious title was inspired by a newspaper advert.
Rod Stewart's cover charted along with his gravelly take on Jimi Hendrix's "Angel".

KANSAS CITY
The Beatles (1964)

This Leiber and Stoller piano shuffle was first aired by the diminutively-titled Little Willie Littlefield way back in 1952. Amongst dozens of subsequent covers it was Little Richard's larger than life version (which he frequently segued with his own "Hey Hey Hey Hey") which put it in the Fabs' early live sets and eventually on to their *Beatles For Sale* album.

BALTIMORE
Nina Simone (1977)

Nina Simone was unhappy with the arrangements on her 1978 album *Baltimore*, which included covers of songs by Daryl Hall and Judy Collins. The title track, a reggaeish amble around Randy Newman's tale of hard living in Maryland's first city, is a slick, upbeat opener.

20-year-old songwriter, Jimmy Webb, it is sung in the first person and tells the story of a man plotting his escape from a failed relationship. It maps, in the protagonist's mind, a drive eastwards from LA, through Arizona to Oklahoma – 1,000 miles – where his new life will flutter, phoenix-life from the ashes. The whole song is set in the future tense: at each stopping point, the singer imagines what the girl he's left behind will be doing – rising, starting work, sleeping. Campbell thought it was an unusual approach to the classic break-up song and sensed a hit. Slowing down the tempo to emphasise the melancholy and sense of anticipation, he recorded his version, making it the opener to his next album. As a single it continued Campbell's run of hits and would be followed by more Webb-penned songs, 'Galveston' and 'Witchita Lineman'.

Although the song ends in Oklahoma, Webb's birthplace, its roots are in Los Angeles. Back in 1965, Webb would walk with his girlfriend, Susan Ronstadt (a cousin of the singer Linda Ronstadt) in LA's MacArthur Park. "We met for lunch and paddleboat rides and feeding the ducks," he told the *Los Angeles Times*. "She worked across the street at a life insurance company." When they broke up it affected Webb badly. He penned two songs for her: 'MacArthur Park' (later hits for Richard Harris and Donna Summer) and 'By the Time I Get to Phoenix'. Webb had never made the trip to Phoenix, however – "I never even got as far as Riverside" – and some have commented on the song's geographic implausibility.

'Phoenix' has been covered by many, most notably in an astonishing 18-minute interpretation by Isaac Hayes on his 1969 album *Hot Buttered Soul*. Hayes builds the tension in a long prologue, setting the scene and providing something of a backstory to the main drama. It's an extraordinary cover version on one of soul's landmark releases. Webb himself has made several recordings of the song, most recently with Campbell reprising his lead vocals and with Mark Knopfler on guitar. Nick Cave also once recorded it, although the Phoenix in his glovebox atlas sounds more like an unwelcoming heart of darkness, somewhere out in the badlands, than Arizona's first city.

YOUNG, GIFTED AND BLACK
BOB AND MARCIA (1970)
Original by Nina Simone (1969)

Inspired by the playwright Lorraine Hansberry, the first black woman to have her work produced on Broadway, the jazz singer and civil rights campaigner Nina Simone wrote 'To Be Young, Gifted and Black' with pianist Weldon Irvine Jr. Simone asked Irvine to contribute the lyrics. "It was the only time in my life that I wrestled with creating," he recalled. When the words finally came, Irvine was in his car. "I tied up traffic at that red light for fifteen minutes, as I scribbled on three napkins and a matchbook cover." The uplifting message of empowerment topped the R&B charts in 1969 and was declared the black national anthem by the Congress of Racial Equality.

Simone's performance encouraged a generation to stand up for their rights. When it comes to dancing, however, it's the version by reggae singers Bob Andy and Marcia Griffiths that gets you on your feet. It was recorded in Jamaica in 1970. "[The producer] Harry J came by with a recording of 'Young, Gifted and Black' and asked me if I'd be interested in voicing it," recalled Andy. "I said I'd give it a try. I invited Marcia to the studio just to accompany me." Trojan Records Anglicised their recording by overdubbing strings, courtesy of arranger Johnny Arthey, and issued it in the UK. Griffiths and Andy gave the release little thought until they received an excited call from Harry J a few weeks later: "'You have to go to England!' And we said why? And he said, 'You have to sing on *Top of the Pops*!'" It was reggae's biggest international hit to date. Bob and Marcia's success with the record paired the two artists for the next four years, until Marcia joined the I-Threes, Bob Marley's backing trio.

The song's composers have led somewhat more unsettled lives

over the last three decades. Embittered by what she saw as the failure of the civil rights movement, an uncompromising Simone renounced her homeland in 1969 and exiled herself in a variety of countries in Africa and Europe. In the 1990s Weldon Irvine became a mentor for the hip-hop generation. Sadly, he committed suicide in New York in 2002, aged 58.

MONEY'S TOO TIGHT (TO MENTION)
SIMPLY RED (1985)
Original by the Valentine Brothers (1982)

Simply Red's recordings of other people's songs tend towards the easy copy (Harold Melvin and the Blue Notes' 'If You Don't Know Me By Now') or the simply dreadful (their doctoring of Gregory Isaacs' intimate 'Night Nurse' tends to bring on nocturnal chills). The Mancunian band's first hit was a blue-eyed reading of this relatively little-known gentle funk cut from the Valentine Brothers. The resume of Ohio-born Billy and John Valentine includes a slew of session work; Billy did time with a jazz outfit, the Young-Holt Unlimited trio, and the two enjoyed a stint touring with the black musical 'The Wiz', before releasing a handful of slick soul albums in the late Seventies and early Eighties under their own name. 'Money's Too Tight', a solid R&B hit for the duo, appeared on their celebrated 1982 set, *First Take*, produced by Bobby Lyle.

The brooding fusion-funk was perfect for the time, fading in on a bass line that firmly shakes your money-maker and lyrics that speak of financial hardship. With references to unemployment and "Reaganomics", the song was chosen by Mick Hucknall for its serendipitous anti-Thatcher sentiments. Back in the Eighties, Simply Red's version sounded as bouncy as a Robert Maxwell pension cheque, but it's barely a nickel-and-dime on the original. Hucknall recorded it early in 1985, after several stalled attempts to launch his band big-time, and boldly proclaimed his intentions to be the "best white soul singer around". He wasn't, but nevertheless it made the Top 20 in June 1985, neatly trailing Simply Red's debut album *Picture Book*.

The success of the Simply Red cover no doubt gave them a little less cause for fiscal complaint, but the Valentine Brothers never quite realised their potential. They helped out with production duties on the Style Council's *The Cost of Loving* album in 1987 and Billy worked as a writer/producer in Los Angeles in the early Nineties, otherwise little has been heard from them since.

TAKE ME TO THE RIVER
TALKING HEADS (1978)
Original by Al Green (1974)

Al Green's collaborations with Memphis producer Willie Mitchell and the Hi Records rhythm section resulted in some of the most soul-stirring sounds of the Seventies. Included on Green's 1974 outing, *Al Green Explores Your Mind*, is the gospel-tinged 'Take Me to the River'. Written with Mabon "Teenie" Hodges, guitarist with the Hi house band, Green's song squares the singer's early religious convictions with more earthly interests. When Green was ordained as the pastor of the Full Gospel Tabernacle Church in 1976, he dropped the song from his repertoire. "As far as the church was concerned I was still singing rhythm and blues," he said in interview. "[The Church felt] if you're serious about what you're doing, you can't sing that anymore... So for eight years I didn't sing any of my music."

'Take Me to the River' remained an album track for Green. Instead it was taken into the R&B charts by Mississippi-born singer Syl Thompson. In 1978 it was a breakthrough single for Talking Heads, also featuring on their second album, *More Songs About Buildings and Food*, produced by Brian Eno. Lead Head David Byrne disassembles Green's original note-by-note, the tempo is slowed and the already loose arrangement laid prone and massaged to the point where it is indistinguishable from one of the Heads' own songs. Crucially, Byrne recreated the song without sacrificing its intrinsic funk. Green approved and jokingly commented that he hoped to cover one of Talking Heads' songs someday. "I thought it was magnificent," he said. "It was a different view, viewing the song from a different perspective." Happily his secular songs have now been back in the Reverend Green's live set for some time. "I went to pray. I went up into the mountains as far as I could go. I went without eating for 21 to 30 days... I was asking about the songs and I was told right then and there: I gave you the songs. Use those songs, sing your songs." We are still awaiting Green's cover of 'Psycho Killer', however.

HEY JOE
JIMI HENDRIX (1966)
Original claimed by Billy Roberts (1962)

It's been covered by everyone from Deep Purple to Patti Smith. Jimi Hendrix's debut hit has a complicated provenance. Composition of this brooding tale of premeditated murder was originally claimed by a West Coast folkie, Billy Roberts, who copyrighted it in 1962. However, the conventional chord structure and similarity to other blues ditties led many to suspect it was much older. Roberts was inconsistent in his explanation of how he came up with such a powerful song. He at first maintained he'd etched the lyrics in the sand on a Maine beach, only committing them to paper years later. Another version of events has Roberts co-writing 'Hey Joe' whilst playing an Edinburgh folk club in 1956. Len Partridge, a leading light in the Scottish postwar folk-blues boom, recalled: "We played quite a lot together and one of the things which came out of that period was 'Hey Joe'... Don't even ask me now which bits were added by me. I can't claim credit for it – that really does have to go to Bill."

Then there is Niela Miller, a girlfriend of Roberts in the late Fifties. She insists that her song 'Baby Please Don't Go To Town' was plagiarised by the folk singer, who altered the lyrics to "Hey Joe, where you goin' with that gun in your hand?" "My music publisher at the time advised me against suing Billy," she said. Lawyer Martin Cohen, who administers the rights to the song, has also doubted Roberts' claim. "It's always been difficult for me to believe that this guy could write this phenomenon," he said. "To my knowledge Roberts never recorded it."

According to Cohen it was first cut by singer Dino Valente (who, confusingly, also assumed co-writing credits for a while and was paid composer's royalties). Until Hendrix, the best-known versions were by Californian pop band the Leaves and gravel-throated troubadour Tim Rose. Rose clearly considered 'Hey Joe' to be his. He added a verse and slowed the tempo for his first album, released in 1966: "I was essentially writing a new song," he claimed. Hendrix picked up on this version either from his manager, Chas Chandler, or from Love's Arthur Lee (in his autobiography Keith Richards claims it was his tape of Rose's demo which was given to Hendrix). Hendrix's 'Hey Joe' twists like a corpse on the gallows. Rose was unimpressed: "I know I'm not the guitar player he was, but I still think my version is better."

HELLO HURRAY
ALICE COOPER (1973)
Original by Judy Collins (1968)

Alice Cooper's third Top 10, a hit in 1973, is as strong as a python and as camp as smudged mascara. 'Hello Hurray' (sometimes 'Hello Hooray') was written on a borrowed guitar beside a swimming pool in a house in Laurel Canyon, LA, in 1968. Its composer, Ontario folk singer Rolf Kempf, recalls: "I was there for the lack of anywhere else to go, since my band had broken up and gone back to Canada, and all my belongings had been stolen, including my guitar." Fellow folkie Judy Collins came around, seeking material for her next album. "She really liked 'Hello Hurray', although it seemed out of character at the time. But she recorded it and did a great job".

It's the life-affirming introduction to her celebrated folk-rock set *Who Knows Where The Time Goes* (as 'Hello, Hooray'), produced by David Anderle and featuring guest artists James Burton, Stephen Stills and Van Dyke Parks. Collins warbles like a whitethroat through lines later excised by Cooper: "Hello, hooray, let the lights grow dim, I've been ready / Ready as the rain to fall, just to fall again / Ready as a man to be born, only to be born again". The song has a spiritual purpose, as Kempf explains: "My inspiration was the concept of self-renewal and re-invention to help me through a frustrating period of my life. And it has helped in more ways than one."

Detroit's premier shock-rocker first heard the song through his producer, Bob Ezrin, who met Kempf at a Toronto party. Released as a single, it reached Number Six in the UK and became the opener to Cooper's extravagant stage show: "I liked the idea of doing a big Anthony Newley-type Broadway thing". It's the least depraved track on Cooper's glam-dram classic, *Billion Dollar Babies*. "The whole idea behind the album," said Alice at the time, "is to exploit the idea that

THE COVER CAME FIRST

Sometimes a song is entrusted to another singer before the writer can get to grips with it themselves. Here are six, cunningly crafted by others ahead of the original.

WILD HORSES
THE ROLLING STONES (1971)

Although it had been recorded in 1970, before gracing *Sticky Fingers* the following year, Gram Parsons grabbed this Jagger and Richards number for his band the Flying Burrito Brothers and snuck it out before the Stones' blueprint. It's since been tamed by many.

OH! YOU PRETTY THINGS
DAVID BOWIE (1971)

Pop's greatest song about Nietzsche and Crowley was first a smiley slice of bubblegum for Herman's Hermits' cheeky-chappy Peter Noone in 1971. Bowie tinkles the ivories on the Noone hit, before releasing his own homo-superior version on the album *Hunky Dory*.

MY SWEET LORD
GEORGE HARRISON (1970)

Demoed by Harrison in the closing weeks of the Sixties, as the Beatles were unravelling, this irresistible devotional anthem was cherry picked by Billy Preston for a gospel handclap on his 1970 album *Encouraging Words*. Harrison's definitive version followed three months later and was a huge hit - the first time most people had heard it.

everyone has sick perversions. But they've got to be American perversions; we're very nationalistic, you know." Kempf was delighted with Cooper's rendition: "He got the emotional essence of the tune right, and added a tag to bring it home." Kempf released a string arrangement of his most famous song on his self-produced 2002 album *Daydreamer* and updated it again in 2009, commenting: "After adapting the song for an athletic event, I realized it really moves well with a Euro/Dance beat".

SHIPBUILDING
ELVIS COSTELLO (1983)
David Bowie cited it as the song he most wished he'd written: "Stunning piece of work; makes me cry, just the opening bars," said Bowie. Written by Costello and Clive Langer for Robert Wyatt, Costello eventually plucked up the courage to record his own version for the 1983 album *Punch the Clock*. "It took me a long time to get the vocal on it, because of being in [Wyatt's] shadow," Elvis said.

FIRE
BRUCE SPRINGSTEEN (2010)
Written in 1977, when the Boss was unable to issue records due to contractual wrangles, this Elvis Presley dedication was first released the following year by Robert Gordon (with Springsteen on keyboards) and taken chartwards by the Pointer Sisters. Springsteen kept the song in his live set and a 1978 concert recording made it to 45 in the Eighties, but his splendid Elvishly studio version had to wait until 2010's *The Promise*.

THESE DAYS
JACKSON BROWNE (1973)
Written when he was just 16, this lilting ballad was first recorded by Browne's then belle Nico, for her 1967 Warhol-inspired album *Chelsea Girl*. Six years later Browne reinterpreted it on his second album *For Everyman*, sounding more denim and cheesecloth than venus in furs. The album also features the songwriter's own version of the Eagles' debut single, 'Take it Easy'.

WILD WORLD
MAXI PRIEST (1988)
Original by Jimmy Cliff (1970)

Maxi Priest cut his teeth with south London's Saxon reggae sound system, before becoming a solo recording artist with international success. This gloriously creamy, carnival favourite, written by Cat Stevens and made famous by Jimmy Cliff 18 years earlier, was a huge hit on both sides of the Atlantic in the summer of 1988.

In 1970, Stevens, aged only 21 and with a fine pop career behind him, was stuck between recording contracts with a classic in his pocket. While he sorted out a signing to Island records, 'Wild World' was given over to someone else, identity unknown. "They just didn't understand what the song was about, they just did it very badly," Stevens later recalled. "So I thought, 'I'll do a backing track to that and find a singer who can really sing'." Stevens put some money down on studio time and co-opted a session trio called Flare to cut the track. He then invited reggae artist Jimmy Cliff down for a listen. Cliff, who came fresh from the charts, riding on the success of his debut hit, 'Wonderful World, Beautiful People', had just the right voice: as fresh and bright as a strawberry. Cat had got the cream: "Jimmy really liked it. He just sang it straight off. It was fantastic. It was meant to be. It was his song."

Like another of Stevens' much-covered songs, 'Father and Son', it's a word of advice from parent to newly-fledged child. "It was a matter of understanding the rat-race of cities and civilizations and societies, whatever it is," analysed Cat. "Just understanding that it is a crazy world, it's a mad world, you know, it has no rules; the only rule is to win". It was a sentiment that Cliff, the rambunctious young singer from Kingston, Jamaica could relate to and one to which he would give full expression in 'The Harder They Come' a couple of years on. "I think Jimmy has had the same kind of experience in his life somewhere along the line."

'Wild World' followed 'Wonderful World, Beautiful People' into the Top 10. Stevens, recast as the Seventies' Donovan, issued his own, equally well-known, version of the song on the meditative long-player *Tea for the Tillerman*. Released on seven-inch in the US only, it made the Billboard charts the following year. "You might think that 'Wild World' was written about some girl," he said at the time. "In fact, [it] was written about me. I was writing to myself, saying that I knew that I was going to turn into what I was before: a pop star."

HUSH
KULA SHAKER (1997)
Original by Billy Joe Royal (1967)

In 1997 Kula Shaker, who were unashamed fans of the early Deep Purple sound, turned one of Purple's first singles into a hit of their own, landing it at Number Two in the UK charts. Their version of 'Hush' was recorded in one shot at LA's Sound City. Kula Shaker's singer and guitarist Crispian Mills sings it like he means it. "He's a really wild player," their producer commented. "He has great technique – the sound is in his fingers."

The song had already been round the block a few times before it wound up with Kula Shaker. Penned by white R&B songwriter Joe South, 'Hush' was initially a hit in 1967 for South's best mate from Valdosta, Georgia: Billy Joe Royal. Royal, around on the country scene since the early Sixties, tuned in to gospel acts like the Staple Singers, southern rhythm and blues and Detroit's driving Motor City sound. "I know exactly what George Jones feels," he once said. "But I know exactly what Ray Charles feels, too." Produced by South, 'Hush' is an amalgam of all these influences: a mid-paced rocker with a down-home soul. The guitars twang, the drums slap and a tambourine rings out like the bell atop a clapboard chapel. There's an irresistible "na-na-na" hook and an impassioned plea from Royal. The narrator has lost his girl, but he might hear her crying for him, if everyone would just keep quiet. After the hit, Royal's career took a dive. "Hard rock came in and I didn't really fit in there anywhere," he said. "Everything was group oriented and all at once there just didn't seem to be a place for me."

But hard rock was just what the song needed. The group who rescued Royal's song was Deep Purple. Guitarist Richie Blackmore first heard it whilst living in Hamburg. "I thought it was a great song, and I also thought it would be a good song to add to our act, if we could come up with a different arrangement," he told one journalist. 'Hush' was given the heavy treatment and included on the band's debut album *Shades of Deep Purple*. Singer Rod Evans lacks Royal's urgent holler, but Blackmore screams through it. "We did the whole song in two takes... There's actually one part where the guitar is feeding back, sustaining. I have a tendency to switch pickups as I'm playing, almost like a nervous habit." Released as a single it established the band in the United States, reaching Number Four in 1968.

WALK THIS WAY
RUN DMC (1986)
Original by Aerosmith (1975)

Although no one would have thought it back in 1975, when it first appeared as a single lifted from the album *Toys in the Attic*, 'Walk This Way' would not only be responsible for salvaging Aerosmith's flagging career ten years later, it would also alter the course of rock music. During rehearsals for the album in the spring of 1975, Steven Tyler, the Boston band's flamboyant singer, put some lyrics to a faltering riff, vaguely inspired by the Yardbirds. Stuck for a title to the new song, the band took some downtime to catch the Mel Brooks horror spoof *Young Frankenstein*. In one scene the comedian Marty Feldman blinked his bulging eyes and muttered the words "Walk this way". The band were in stitches. They had their title.

Aerosmith took off, but by the mid Eighties were pretty much grounded in a haze of drug and money problems. Tyler was living off a small allowance from his manager and doing his best to sidestep repo and rehab. Guitarist and co-composer of the song, Joe Perry, had temporarily quit the band in 1980 and it took a new manager, Tim Collins, to navigate them through their legal tussles and get them signed to Geffen Records.

Over in New York City, Run DMC had, apparently, never heard of Aerosmith, although they were familiar with the opening break to 'Walk This Way', which rappers such as Grandmaster Flash had often used. "None of them had actually heard the song," said their producer, Rick Rubin, who grew up on rock 'n' roll and first played them the record. "[I always knew] that there was this connection between rock and rap," he said. "One had guitars, one usually didn't." Rubin suggested they cut a cover. His suggestion was initially met with raised eyebrows from Run DMC. After scrutinising the lyrics,

"We said, this is hillbilly gibberish," they later told *Rolling Stone* magazine. Rubin picked up the phone and Tyler was invited down to record the chorus. "Then Run did the rhymes and then Steven joined in." It worked. A crossover hit called. "We already had MTV in our grasp," said Rubin. "'Walk This Way' just came and grabbed the world." Their collaborative remake was a global hit. It is credited for breaking down the wall between hip-hop and rock (literally, in the video to the song) and resurrecting Aerosmith's career. None was more pleased than Rubin. "It showed people that rap was 'music'."

HOLD BACK THE NIGHT
GRAHAM PARKER AND THE RUMOUR (1977)
Original by the Trammps (1975)

The Trammps, best remembered now perhaps for their ubiquitous 'Disco Inferno', actually enjoyed their biggest British chart success with this Philly groove in 1975. Formed three years earlier by drummer and bass-vocalist Earl Young, the Trammps comprised ex-members of Sixties soul strutters the Volcanos and top session players seconded from Kenny Gamble and Leon Huff's Philly International house band. "They were kinda raggedy when I first got them together," Young recalled. "So the Trammps was a pretty appropriate name to call them." 'Hold Back the Night', the group's third dance-floor hit, began life as 'Scrub Board', an instrumental B-side. Recut with the soaring vocal talents of Jimmy Ellis, it hustled and bumped its way into the Top 10 and caught the ear of the London-born R&B singer and one-time Mod, Graham Parker, who was struggling for a hit with some splendid, but commercially unsuccessful, self-penned material.

Parker and his band the Rumour talked among themselves: "A few Neanderthal grunts served as pointers and defining moments in the art of solidifying musical arrangements, set-lists and hairstyles," he said. "Somehow in this ethereal stew of non-communication I must have broached the idea of covering 'Hold Back the Night', and somehow the idea must have been accepted." Parker taped it at Cologne's Dierks studio during a European tour. The Rumour's front man, Brinsley Schwarz, was on sick leave with jaundice: his shoes were filled by Thin Lizzy's harmony-guitarist Brian Robertson. Their arrangement of 'Hold Back the Night', as snug as an Italian three-button, appeared on the lurid vinyl *Pink Parker* EP early in 1977. That the original version was still keeping glitter-balls spinning at soul weekenders around the country did not bother Parker. His intention was "merely to fill in the gap between albums in the time-honoured tradition of EPs, like the Stones and the Beatles used to do".

'Hold Back the Night' provided Parker and the Rumour with long-awaited chart success, peaking at Number 24. In 1992 the Trammps, far from down-and-out, leant their vocals to the short-lived Nottingham dance trio KWS (Chris King, Winnie Williams and Delroy St Joseph) for a House version of the song, which shuffled in to the lower reaches of the Top 30.

GO NOW
MOODY BLUES (1964)
Original by Bessie Banks (1963)

You had to be resourceful to get a hit in 1964. Unless your beat combo had a Paul McCartney or Ray Davies on board, the trick was to find something in the local import racks from the American R&B charts and re-record it. The more obscure the better. Birmingham's Moody Blues found 'Go Now', by Bessie Banks. "It was a very slow blues number, not very well known the time," recalled the Moody's original bass player, Clint Warwick (baptised with the distinctly un-hip name of Albert Eccles). This valedictory ballad was written by Larry Banks, of the Four Fellows singing group, and Milton Bennett. Bessie's proud vocal follows an irresistible sequence of piano chords, each one plunging us further into despair. In two and half minutes the song tears the listener apart.

The Moody Blues brought 'Go Now' to London's Marquee club, where they had begun a residency in mid 1964. "It was the piano start that we liked; so we kept that. We played it in the same style as Bessie Banks," Warwick recalled. "It went down well, so we thought we would record it. There was a studio just being built at the back of the Marquee, so we recorded it there." Vocalist Denny Laine chases the same piano riff, played by Mike Pinder, but this time there's a stronger beat and a more buxom sound. "We had to do it our way. It took us a long time."

They were on a Chuck Berry tour when 'Go Now' hit the charts and, unexpectedly, shot to Number One in early 1965. "After that we toured with the Beatles, staying at castles and mansions – Brian Epstein never put his band up at town hotels," recalls Warwick. "We got to know them quite well. They were good mates. McCartney was always at our house, getting our opinions on songs." But the Moody Blues were unable to repeat their early success and by 1966 they were as good as broke. For Warwick and Laine, it was indeed time to go now. Laine went solo, eventually teaming up with his old Beatle pal in Wings (who also released a concert version of 'Go Now'), and Warwick said goodbye to the music business altogether. They were replaced by two knights in white satin, Justin Hayward and John Lodge.

GOT MY MIND SET ON YOU
GEORGE HARRISON (1987)
Original by James Ray (1961)

George Harrison was the first Beatle to set foot on American soil. In September 1963 he spent a fortnight with his sister Louise, a resident of Benton, a small mining town in southern Illinois. George wandered the trim streets, checked out the stores and even made a booking for his band at the local country club (by the time the Beatles made it to the States, however, they were too big to play Benton). He returned to Britain with a Rickenbacker 425 and a copy of a James Ray 45, 'Got My Mind Set on You'.

Ray was a former GI from Washington D.C. Once his draft was through he picked up his singing career and aimed it at the soulful end of rhythm and blues. He was living rough when producer Gerry Granahan urged him into the studio. "Got My Mind Set on You", penned by the prolific songwriter Rudy Clark, was recorded by Ray in 1961. It skips around the yard to a bouncing, reggae-style beat, this lightweight tale of woe. The Beatles had already included Ray's better-known 'If You Gotta Make a Fool of Somebody' in their live set, before leaving Freddie and the Dreamers to kick that one into the charts. It's unlikely they considered 'Got My Mind Set on You', but the song stuck with Harrison.

In 1987 the Quiet One was working on his third album of the Eighties at his home studio in Henley, and he was in retro mode. Ringo was behind the drums once more and Clapton was sitting in on guitar. *Cloud Nine* was, in part, a finely-crafted, nostalgic look back to the Beatle years, "when we was fab", as he wryly put it. Harrison no doubt nudged his mind back even further, to the days when he could still walk the streets of any British or American town unhindered. And he remembered that record by James Ray. Harrison's cover of

'Got My Mind Set on You', arranged with the help of producer Jeff Lynne, lost some of the original lyrics but otherwise is a vast improvement, a sweet piece of positive pop. Released as a single, it jumped to the top of the charts, providing him with his biggest hit since 'My Sweet Lord'.

WAR
EDWIN STARR (1970)
Original by the Temptations (1970)

In 1970 Tamla Motown was still catching up with the decade it had just left behind. Buried on the Temptations' album of that year, *Psychedelic Shack*, which came packaged in a cartoon house and flower-power slogan, was what would become the label's best-known protest song. 'War' was an attempt by producer Norman Whitfield and lyricist Barrett Strong to give mainstream black music a voice in the opposition to Vietnam. It snaps to attention with an incontrovertible call-and-response. Say it again. Whitfield's arrangement was planned with military precision: horns explode at just the right moments, the percussion chops like helicopter blades and the boys in the line keep time with an indefatigable "Hup, two, three, four", behind Dennis Edwards' strident lead vocal.

It caught the mood of the time and peace campaigners, mostly students, petitioned Motown to release it as a single. But label boss Berry Gordy was uneasy at the new political slant of his flagship act. Enter minor Motown artist, Edwin Starr. Starr hadn't recorded anything in six months: when Whitfield put him forward for a cover of 'War', to appease the college kids, he was delighted. "It was a message record, an opinion record, and stepped beyond being sheer entertainment," Starr said. "It could become a smash record, and that was fine, but if it went the other way, it could kill the career of whoever the artist was." Edwin was prepared to take the risk. Hedging his bets, however, he maintained that his lyrics were in fact a plea for an end to the gang rivalry that had sparked riots in Chicago and Los Angeles. "It never once mentioned the war in Vietnam. It just so happened that, at the time, the war was going on, and the words just lent themselves to the occasion. Actually, we were talking about a war of people."

Included on his 1970 album *War & Peace*, Starr's version was the pacifist anthem of the year, reaching beyond the college constituency to shift more than three million copies and earn the singer a Grammy nomination. It was later covered by the Jam, Frankie Goes to Hollywood and Bruce Springsteen. Vietnam rumbled on for another five years, but 'War' was undoubtedly Starr's greatest moment. "Afterward, I recorded another song called 'Stop the War Now'," he recalled. "I didn't like that song. I thought it was much too similar."

LOVE HURTS
GRAM PARSONS (1973)
Original by the Everly Brothers (1960)

There may be as many versions of 'Love Hurts' as there have been broken hearts. First recorded by Don and Phil Everly for the 1960 album, *A Date with the Everly Brothers*, it's been covered by countless country and rock artists. It was written by Boudleaux Bryant, a veteran country composer and former Radio Cowboy from Shellman, Georgia. Together with his songwriting partner and wife, Felice, Bryant gave the Everlys many of their early hits. "I learned more from them than from anybody," Don Everly has said. "Boudleaux was a great philosophic teacher."

The brothers loved the song and wanted it out as a single. But the dismissal of their manager, Wesley Rose, in a dispute over song publishing, lost them access to the necessary permissions, so it remained an album track. The first memorable cover of the great lost Everlys single was Roy Orbison's soaring falsetto performance, the B-side to his 1961 hit, 'Running Scared'. In Orbison's hands, 'Love Hurts' is transformed from maudlin self pity into a noble song of experience. As an A-side it has twice troubled the UK charts. In 1975 Traffic drummer Jim Capaldi rushed through a cheerful, breakneck version. Cher's mawkish 1991 attempt, conversely, was scuppered by over-production.

'Love Hurts' found its natural home with another cowboy from the state of Georgia. Gram Parsons rerouted country music with his 1973 album, *Grievous Angel*, which featured the definitive version of 'Love Hurts'. After a year touring coast-to-coast and a fortnight off the bottle, his weather-beaten voice had never sounded better. In the band are a couple of Presley sidemen and Al Perkins on pedal steel. A young Emmylou Harris provides exquisite harmony. "Our singing came together... on 'Love Hurts'," Harris said. "I finally learned what I was supposed to do." Two months after the album's completion, Parsons took his Jaguar and a stash of drugs for a final drive through the twisted rock and waving yuccas, up to California's high desert. He died of an overdose at the Joshua Tree Inn in September 1973. A live duet of 'Love Hurts', recorded with Emmylou, was nominated for a posthumous Grammy in 1983.

I HEARD IT THROUGH THE GRAPEVINE
MARVIN GAYE (1968)
Original by the Miracles (1966)

'I Heard it Through the Grapevine', a tense and troubled rebuttal to cheating love, was written in 1967 on a $40 piano with only ten working keys. By late 1968 it had already done the rounds at Motor City, having been recorded first by the Miracles and the Isley Brothers before Gladys Knight and the Pips took it into the Billboard charts. It was co-writer Norman Whitfield who finally persuaded Motown's boss, Berry Gordy, that what 'Grapevine' really needed was Marvin Gaye. Gaye had already recorded an earlier version, which had been shelved, but Whitfield's faith in the song and the singer never failed. "Norman believed in it so strongly he almost lost his job," recalled co-writer Barrett Strong. Whitfield got his second chance.

Slowing the tempo on the Gladys Knight version, Whitfield builds the intro around a muted piano, solitary cymbal and rattle-snake tambourine, before the drums roll in on a murmur of quivering strings and Chinese whispers, straight from a suspense thriller. "Norman had this whole new arrangement worked out and it came out pretty good," said Gaye. "I wasn't into myself as an artist. I was into being produce-able. I simply took Norman's direction as I felt the direction he was expounding was a proper one." Gaye's vocal was a triumph: "I was reaching for notes that made my veins bulge".

Second time around, Whitfield and Strong's 'Grapevine' actually made it out of the bodega and was slated for Gaye's 1968 offering, *In The Groove*, but it was soon picked up and given air play as more than just an album filler. Released on seven-inch in early 1969 it eventually sold over two and a half million copies, becoming Motown's most successful single and elevating Gaye's career to a new pitch. "When people heard 'Grapevine' they said 'This is a phenomenal artist, he can do anything'," said Strong. Gaye himself was typically self-effacing, tipping his hat to Whitfield and Strong. "Had I [written] the song myself I would not have sung it at all like that, but there are many benefits in just singing other people's material and taking directions," said Gaye. "The job of interpreting is quite an important one because when people are not able to express what is in their souls, and there is an artist who can, then I think that is very valuable."

SUPERSTITION
JEFF BECK (1973)
Original by Stevie Wonder (1972)

Talking Book, Stevie Wonder's elegant, soft soul masterpiece, was recorded at New York's Electric Lady studios in summer 1972. London's premier rock guitarist, Jeff Beck, accepted an invitation to play on a couple of tracks. "I couldn't really be bothered with white rock 'n' roll anymore," recalled Beck. "I was definitely into the black roots and funk. Dirty funk, you know – real electric funk." The deal was, for a contribution or two from the guitar virtuoso, Wonder would provide one song, "to get me going, you know, in that new direction". Beck duly laid down his smooth solo on "Looking for Another Pure Love" and pressed Wonder for his side of the bargain.

"So one day, Stevie says 'Ok, I'll write you a song for you'," Wonder's recording engineer, Malcolm Cecil, told the authors of *The Billboard Book of Number 1 R&B Hits*. From another room Wonder heard Beck fooling around on the drums. "He came in and said 'don't stop'," recalled Beck. Wonder sat at the clavinet and between them they gave birth to the groove for what would become 'Superstition'. "I even helped out with the lyrics," claimed Beck. Cecil claims he sent his charge off to another room to dictate the lines to a secretary.

FURTHER LISTENING

It was the label that launched the Sound of Young America, built on the huge writing talents of Holland-Dozier-Holland, Smokey Robinson and Stevie Wonder. Here are six more takes on Tamla.

THE TEARS OF A CLOWN
THE BEAT (1979)
One of 2-Tone's early signings put the reggae backbeat into Smokey Robinson's 1970 Number One. Ranking Roger's talkover gave the recording that essential ska slant.

PLEASE MR POSTMAN
THE BEATLES (1963)
The Marvelettes' 1961 Tamla cut was taken to market in the UK by the Beatles who put it into their early live act and recorded it for *With The Beatles*. It was later revived by the Carpenters in a chirpy, chart-friendly version.

I WANT YOU BACK
SHERYL CROWE (2010)
Recorded as a tribute to the late Michael Jackson, one of the Corporation's best compositions for Motown's junior signing in the late Sixties. Also covered by Graham Parker.

YOU CAN'T HURRY LOVE
PHIL COLLINS (1982)
Back in the day, when ABC heard Smokey sing and Spandau Ballet listened to Marvin all night long, this global hit became the definitive Motown song for many Eighties listeners.

KEEP ME HANGIN' ON
VANILLA FUDGE (1967)
Pounding, head-banging version of the contemporary H-D-H hit by the Supremes. Committed to tape by the band in one take and these days much used in movie soundtracks.

MERCY MERCY
ROBERT PALMER (1991)
Never a huge UK hit in the hands of its originator, this smooth, late-night dinner party take on one of Motown's key releases (coupled with the Marvin Gaye track 'I Want You'), pushed the former Vinegar Joe singer firmly into the Top 10.

Spontaneous genius was at work. "I was thinking about the beat and I was thinking about Stax, you know the drums and everything, and the groove," said Wonder. Back in the control room the spiky-haired guitarist was told, to his delight, that this was his song. The track was as funky as a feather cut.

Whatever Wonder had in mind when he played Beck 'Superstition', Motown had other plans. "That song was so monstrous that [they told Wonder], 'That ain't for Jeff Beck – that's for you'," the guitarist recalled. Under label pressure, Wonder reneged on his handshake and his recording of 'Superstition' was issued as the first single from *Talking Book*. "That was the right decision, but we were gutted, you know, totally," said Beck. The Motown star made peace by offering 'Cause We've Ended As Lovers' for Beck's album *Blow by Blow*.

In 1973, with Wonder's original in and out of the charts, Beck was free to cut his own version of 'Superstition'. He did so with his band Beck, Bogart and Appice. Beck's serpentine guitar wraps the song up in one of the hardest funk-grooves this side of Hendrix. "Our lyrics are a little different than Stevie's version," commented the drummer Carmine Appice. It's one of the greatest of covers and a glimpse at how we would perhaps know the song now had Gordy not put a block on Beck.

A NEW ENGLAND
KIRSTY MACCOLL (1984)
Original by Billy Bragg (1983)

As mining communities were riven by all-out strike in 1984, the former soldier and one-man punk band Billy Bragg toured the country, playing benefits and penning political diatribes. Kirsty MacColl recognised a songsmith of considerable talent. "He just got up on stage with his guitar and a tiny little amp and sang. I thought, this bloke's brilliant," she recalled. As luck would have it, Bragg was a big fan of MacColl's and was delighted when she asked if she could cover his song 'A New England', which first appeared on Bragg's album *Life's A Riot With Spy Vs Spy*, recorded at Warner Chappell's studios in 1983. "I always thought [it] would be great with loads of harmonies, it's such a good melody. Billy does it in a very rough way and it's like a busker doing a really good Beatles song," she said.

There was one problem: the song wasn't long enough. "Billy had these ideas that he'd thought about using but hadn't got around to doing, so he brought them over to me," she recalled. Bragg scribbled and MacColl bolted on a new, bespoke verse. 'A New England' is a tender love song, in which Bragg's agitprop is put on hold while boy seeks girl – in MacColl's harmony-driven version the line becomes a question: "Are you looking for a new girl?"

The memorable opening couplet was taken from Simon and Garfunkel's folksy 'Leaves that are Green', found on their 1966 album *Sounds of Silence*: "I was 21 years when I wrote this song / I'm 22 now but I won't be for long." Bragg wasn't too worried about borrowing from the acoustic duo. "I didn't really think that anybody would ever hear it. It never crossed my mind," he claimed.

Bragg has continued to play it live. Despite the banner-waving, his fans are generally a quiet lot. "The only time I had trouble there was when a guy jumped out of the audience during 'A New England'," Bragg told one interviewer, recalling a gig in Australia. "He took the mike off me and began singing 'I don't want to change the world, I just want to go to England'. The security guys pounced on him and punched him out."

MYSTERY TRAIN
ELVIS PRESLEY (1955)
Original by Little Junior Parker (1953)

As cover artists go, Elvis Presley – like Sinatra – was one of the most active, relying almost entirely throughout his recording career on cherry-picking other people's songs. But this one was special. This was the song that brought Presley to Sun records, his first label. For that reason alone, it stands as one of the most important postwar recordings. In 1953, Elvis was a driver for the Memphis Crown Electric Company, delivering appliances and listening to a local man, Herman "Little Junior" Parker, on the truck radio. 'Mystery Train' was Parker's current R&B hit. The spectral, hypnotic song, built around a steady, loping rhythm, actually sounds like a steam train: 16 funereal-black coaches carrying his baby off, as Parker says. Raymond Hill's honking saxophone blows like a train whistle and Pat Hare's electric guitar puffs along with precision engineering. Parker's cool vocal brings it to the run-out with a "tsshhh", imitating the brakes. If George Stephenson had made records instead of building steam trains, they would most probably have sounded like this.

Written by Parker, with Sun's president, Sam Phillips, it was the first major hit for the small label. "It was a feeling song," Phillips said. "I mean, it was a big thing, to put a loved one on a train: are they leaving you forever? Maybe they'll never be back." Presley was curious. "He really liked it and chased down where it was done and all this stuff," recalled Phillips. "He later told me that was the main reason he got up enough courage to come in and ask if he could make a record." The song would have to wait another year for him to cover it, in a faster, more spontaneous version, with an extra verse and a groove borrowed from 'Love Me Baby', the flip side of the original Parker single.

It was Presley's fifth and final release for Sun, in the summer of 1955. Presley felt he had paid his dues. Gone were Parker's gimmicky train sounds, replaced with the tangy guitar of Scotty Moore, Bill Black's piston-pumping bass and a springy production that added to the ethereal quality of the song. Elvis broke into a bubbly laugh at the end of the take, thinking he'd screwed up. Phillips knew he'd cut one of the finest rockabilly performances of the era: "It was the greatest thing I ever did on Elvis," he said. These days, the producer can't choose between Presley's and Parker's recordings: "You sit down right now and listen to the contrast of the two, and if you don't like both versions, there's just something bad wrong with you."

FURTHER LISTENING

According to the biographies Presley never wrote a song, although he was granted a co-credit on many, no doubt for royalty advantages. Mostly he relied on professional songwriters and other artists for source material. Here are six classic covers from the King.

SUSPICIOUS MINDS (1969)

The original, by its composer, Mark James, was a flop in 1968. When it was brought to Presley's attention by the producer Chips Moman, the King knew he could do a better job, which he surely did at American Sound Studio, during legendary sessions which spawned the triumphant *From Elvis in Memphis* album.

THE WONDER OF YOU (1970)

Written by Baker Knight and a hit first for Ray Peterson in 1959, it was covered by many before landing at the gates of Graceland in 1970. Presley never made a studio recording of it, however, only ever performing it live in concert.

ARE YOU LONESOME TONIGHT? (1960)

Presley may have heard this 1920s waltz in a 1959 version by chanteuse Jaye P. Morgan, whilst he was serving abroad in the US Army. He based his recording, with the spoken bridge, on the genteel cover by Blue Barron and his Orchestra. His famous "laughter" version was taped live in 1969.

HOUND DOG
ELVIS PRESLEY (1956)
Original by Big Mama Thornton (1952)

One morning Jerry Leiber greeted his songwriting partner Mike Stoller with a smile. "He said, 'we've got a smash hit'," Stoller recalls. "I said, no kidding: what was that. He said 'Hound Dog'. I said, Big Mama Thornton's record? Jerry said: 'No, some white kid named Elvis Presley.' I said, Elvis who?"

ONE NIGHT (1957)
Originally a hit, under the title 'One Night (of Sin)' for Fats Domino soundalike Smiley Lewis in 1957. Elvis trialled a version the same year, but found it too risqué and abandoned it. He made it a hit by reworking the lyrics the following year – presumably with the permission of the song's composers, who included Dave Bartholomew, the man who had penned 'Ain't That a Shame' with Domino and 'I Hear You Knocking' (later covered by Dave Edmunds).

AN AMERICAN TRILOGY (1972)
A portmanteau song from the pen of one of America's most neglected singer-songwriters, Mickey Newbury, combining themes from three nineteenth-century songs. These are 'Dixie', 'All My Trials' and the Civil War march, 'The Battle Hymn of the Republic'. The haunting, ethereal original first appeared on Newbury's 1971 album *Frisco Mabel Joy*.

BLUE SUEDE SHOES (1956)
When Presley signed to RCA, this rock and roll standard was the first song they wanted him to record. This was perhaps no surprise – in 1956 alone over twenty versions appeared from as many different artists. It was penned by Carl Perkins, from a title suggested to him by Johnny Cash. Perkins told Cash, "I don't know anything about shoes. How can I write a song about shoes?"

When Leiber and Stoller first saw Willie Mae "Big Mama" Thornton burst into song, the two teenage Tin Pan Alley writers were moved to pen an instant classic. "'Hound Dog' was written and inspired by Big Mama's physical self and demeanor," says Leiber. "She seemed very tough and salty and angry." They took their song to Johnny Otis, a West Coast bandleader. "They were kids, and they said, we write songs, maybe we can do some things together," Otis told the writer Charlie Gillett. They got to work on the blues shuffle that was 'Hound Dog', backing up Big Mama's gargantuan vocals with plenty of rough-house guitar. "We got it in one take," Stoller said. "We were thrilled. I don't remember being thrilled too many times in the 50 years we've been in this business, but that was thrilling."

'Hound Dog' was first issued on Don Robey's Peacock Records in 1953. But there was a problem. "The next thing we knew, Willie Mae Thornton's version was out, as we'd written it, but with Johnny's name on it," said Stoller. Robey had made an error. "It didn't have Leiber and Stoller's name on it, although it should have," admitted Otis. Leiber and Stoller went to court to straighten things out, ensuring that whoever's name was on the record, they got the money. It sold two million copies, although Thornton allegedly only ever received a cheque for $500. The song would have languished in the rhythm and blues archives, were it not for a young country kid from Mississippi.

Presley's manager, the irrepressible Colonel Tom Parker, had acquired half the publishing rights to the song and Otis was cut out of the credits. "That was the validation that we needed,

'cos we knew we had made that record," says Leiber. Initially the duo hated Presley's rock 'n' roll rendition: "I never thought he was singing the blues. I thought he was singing songs. Somewhat folk, somewhat country, and a little bit of black," says Leiber. "But it grew on me. Like a million-dollar bond."

MY BOY LOLLIPOP
MILLIE SMALL (1964)
Original by Barbie Gaye (1956)

Generally regarded as the first international reggae hit, Millie's 'My Boy Lollipop' actually began life as a shuffling sax-honker by the rhythm and blues singer Barbie Gaye. Composition was credited to Johnny Roberts and record company man Morris Levy, although Bobby Spencer, once of the doo-wop outfit the Cadillacs, is generally recognised as the song's writer. Gaye's original is delivered an octave or so below Millie's shrill signature version. It was a local hit in New York in 1956 and soon made its way over to Jamaica, where a new sound inspired by American R&B was spilling out of the dancehalls: ska.

The teenage Millie was, in 1963, Jamaica's latest ska star, the "blue beat girl" with a couple of hits under her tiny belt. She was picked up by the record producer Chris Blackwell while scouting out new talent for his new venture, Island Records, although her rendition of 'Lollipop' was released in the UK via the mainstream Fontana, for maximum exposure.

It was recorded at London's Olympic Studios in March 1964 and featured only two Jamaican musicians – the legendary guitarist Ernest Ranglin, who also arranged the song for Blackwell, and Pete Peterson on trumpet. Backing was supplied by a Birmingham band, the Five Dimensions, with whom a young Rod Stewart took the mike for a short period in 1964. Stewart's apparent resemblance at the time to a local session player, Pete Hogman, seems to given rise to a much-repeated rumour that he played the harmonica solo on the recording. Hogman, however, is confident it is he and not Stewart on the instrument.

Blackwell used all available resources to achieve the same tone quality he naturally found in studios back in Jamaica. "The reverb came from a sort of cupboard in the back of the studio that we used as a live chamber," he recalled. "It was a mono record, and we fed the sound in, adding a bit more of the reverb on Millie's voice." Cleverly marketed as a novelty disc, 'My Boy Lollipop' propelled the teenager to short-term stardom. She appeared on *Juke Box Jury*, played the Cavern and even cut a version in German. The record lasts the statutory two minutes: "That was important for people at radio who were putting playlists together," said Blackwell. "Millie's voice was irresistible – for a certain length of time, anyway."

I FEEL FOR YOU
CHAKA KHAN (1984)
Original by Prince (1979)

Chaka Khan's rap and slap-bass cover of this little-known Prince song was the first to bring a hip-hop awareness to her brand of patent-leather dance music. Prince's original from 1979, on which he plays all the instruments, is an undernourished, bony-legged disco filler. Three years later the Pointer Sisters fleshed it out in a version for their album *So Excited*, produced by Richard Perry, which hinted at the song's potential. It may have gone no further had Prince not loved what he had heard of Khan: "What a voice this woman has!" he commented. At the Purple One's request, a tape of the song was sent to Arif Mardin, Khan's producer and all-round mentor, with the suggestion that it might fit her profile.

Where others heard hand-claps and a cheesy keyboard riff, Mardin heard a bubbling bass, wailing harmonica and syncopated rapping, all jostling to a boisterous electro-funk arrangement, and he booked some studio time. Prince was down to play guitar, but had to pull out. Stevie Wonder was invited to play harmonica and agreed: his part was recorded in Los Angeles on the day of Marvin Gaye's funeral. Khan taped her vocals in one night. It sounded great, but Mardin needed

FURTHER LISTENING

Prince is one of the most covered songwriters (so many there is a website devoted to listing them). Here are six more from the Purple pen.

I WANNA BE YOUR LOVER
CORINNE BAILEY RAE (2011)
From *The Love EP,* a cover of the lead single from Prince's funky second album - the one which established his signature sound, way back in 1979.

KISS
ART OF NOISE FEATURING TOM JONES (1988)
The Welsh wizard teamed up with avant-garde synth-popsters to take on a brave cover of this 1986 Prince and the Revolution hit.

RASPBERRY BERET
HINDU LOVE GODS (1990)
A loose, rocking version by REM with Warren Zevon sitting in for Michael Stipe. The band's self titled, and only, album was apparently a drunken studio jam and not intended for release.

WHEN DOVES CRY
PATTI SMITH (2001)
A sensual cover of the *Purple Rain* classic, recorded in 2001 and issued as a single to promote the compilation *Land 1975-2002.*

ALPHABET STREET
THE JESUS AND MARY CHAIN (1994)
Drowning in feedback and fuzz, Prince's 1988 sprightly funk gets a clamorous makeover in this bonus track for the relatively tune-friendly JAMC single "Come On".

U GOT THE LOOK
GARY NUMAN (1992)
Bathed in synths and screeching guitar, the original sounds like perfect Numan material. Covered on the album *Machine + Soul*, along with a version of '1999'.

something more. Warner Bros had already invested two albums in the former Rufus front-woman but, despite a couple of hits, things were slowing down. Mardin felt it was time for Khan to start listening to the sound of young America.

The producer tracked down Melle Mel, a rapper with Grandmaster Flash, at Sugarhill Studios and recorded him announcing "Chaka Khan/Chaka Khan", mimicking a drumbeat. Khan hated it. "He played me this guy repeating my name over and over again," she said. "I was so embarrassed. I thought it was horrible." But she liked the song and trusted her producer. Mel's line, intended for the middle of the song, eventually gave the version its trademark opening. "My engineer, Lou Hahn [said] 'I think you should really put this earlier'," Mardin said. "Then it became like a bookend." 'I Feel for You' did its job, getting maximum airplay and reaching the top of the charts on both sides of the Atlantic.

STORMY MONDAY
BOBBY 'BLUE' BLAND (1962)
Original by Earl Hines (1942)

Elvis Costello told us we were 'Welcome to the Working Week'. The fellow in the Easybeats' song clocked-on to his dead-end job with Friday on his mind. For Aaron Thibeaux "T-Bone" Walker it's not just the job: his girl has left him and now he can barely get out of bed. "They call it Stormy Monday / Tuesday's just as bad", Walker wails, as he works his way through the worst week of his life. "Wednesday's worse / Thursday's oh so sad". On Friday the eagle flies – in other words his pay, dollar bills brandishing the American eagle, gets spent on something to cure his hangdog circumstance. On Sunday he's on his knees at church, praying for his baby to come home. How bad does it get?

Walker, a Texan blues showman, wrote 'Stormy Monday' in the early Forties. Composition is occasionally credited to Billy Eckstein, the Forties baritone, and pianist Earl Hines (sometimes with the inclusion of arranger Bob Crowder), who recorded a version as early as 1942 and introduced it to the big-band fraternity. Walker issued the first electric guitar arrangement, in 1947 for the Black & White label, under the supervision of arranger Ralph Bass. For most blues and rock performers his is the blueprint, all muted trumpet and fluttering piano, Walker's Gibson turning notes like a storm-cock in a stiff breeze. Hardly a tempest, but then this is the blues. Titled variously 'Call it Stormy Monday' and 'Stormy Monday Blues', it's been given a run through by countless players and singers over the last six decades.

Walker's version prompted B.B. King to take out a loan on his first guitar, but it was another bluesman, Bobby Bland, who brought the song to the mainstream. His take on 'Stormy Monday', for the 1962 album *Here's the Man*, resurrects the big-band sound in a line-up including fellow musicians Wayne Bennett, Hamp Simmons and John "Jabo" Starks. "[It] was supposed to be a 'throwaway' tune," recalled Starks. "We had already finished the album, and Bobby said, 'Hey, man, I want to do that tune. Let's do that tune, just for me'." In two takes, the rhythm section had it taped. Bennett copied Walker's guitar part and Bland makes it sound like no-one could hate Mondays quite so much.

BIG YELLOW TAXI
COUNTING CROWS (2002)
Original by Joni Mitchell (1969)

Counting Crows were formed in San Francisco in 1991 around the talents of singer Adam Duritz and guitarist David Bryson. Their cover of Joni Mitchell's 'Big Yellow Taxi' was first hidden on the band's 2002 album *Hard Candy* as an uncredited bonus track. With additional vocals by Vanessa Carlton it was edited down for single release, providing the band with their biggest UK hit. It was, perhaps, an odd choice of song, being one of the paradigmatic Sixties protest anthems, but Counting Crows play it like a twenty-first-century original. Nevertheless, it is rooted like a tree in the late-Sixties counterculture – before those trees were put into a tree museum, of course.

Rewind to Hawaii, 1969. Joni Mitchell steps onto her balcony and squints at the Pacific palms. Then she glances down at the concrete car park in the hotel grounds. "I thought 'They paved paradise and put up a parking lot'," she recalled in the early Seventies. "And that's how the song 'Big Yellow Taxi' was born." Mitchell also said she was thinking of another hotel, the Garden of Allah, a swish LA stopover for stars such as Humphrey Bogart and Frank Sinatra, famously torn down in 1950 to make way for a bank and its parking lot. The song's ecological message turns out to be a red herring, though. What's she's really saying is that her old man's left her (Counting Crows deftly altered the line to "my girl"). In the final verse, the screen door slams and off he goes in a large banana-coloured cab. The moral is the same, however. Look after what's yours: you don't know what you've got 'til it's gone.

Mitchell took the completed song to A&M Studios in Hollywood for her third album, *Ladies of the Canyon*. Her swooping vocal delivery, one of the few 22-note melodic spans in popular music, is backed by an open-tuned acoustic guitar, congas, a gourd and finger cymbals. Stripped of any ornamentation, Mitchell once said it had "too much melody". Covers came quickly. A group called the Neighborhood first made it a US hit and Bob Dylan cut a version during sessions for his 1970 album *New Morning* (although it wasn't released until 1973). Janet Jackson lifted a generous sample for her chart-topper 'Got 'Til It's Gone' – with Mitchell's blessing because, allegedly, Jackson once spoke favourably of her album *Chalk Mark in a Rainstorm*.

Despite the twist in the song's close, it's usually thought of as a sort of update on 'Where Have all the Flowers Gone?'. It's not her greatest composition by miles of aisles, but Mitchell is happy with the way it has taken on a life of its own. Certainly she doesn't consider her original to be definitive. "I like the song 'Big Yellow Taxi' better than I like my rendition of it," she once said. "It's a good little workhorse of a song and it's got some content. But it's a nursery rhyme."

Counting Crows clearly like a cover or two. In 2012 they released *Underwater Sunshine*, a covers collection of songs "both familiar and obscure", from Teenage Fanclub's 'Start Again' to Big Star's 'The Ballad of El Goodo' and the Fairport Convention classic 'Meet on the Ledge'.

WITH A LITTLE HELP FROM MY FRIENDS
JOE COCKER (1968)
Original by the Beatles (1967)

The "Ringo track" was a necessary fan-pleasing component of Beatles' albums. For *Sgt Pepper*, Paul McCartney and John Lennon gave their drummer a grown-up children's song to flatten his vowels around. McCartney claims 'With a Little Help From My Friends' started life at Lennon's house in Weybridge, under the working title 'Bad Finger Boogie'. One writing session, however, was witnessed by the band's biographer, Hunter Davies, at Macca's London home. "Whenever they got stuck, they would go back and do a rock 'n' roll song or an Engelbert Humperdinck song and just bugger around," Davies wrote. Lennon contributed the line "What do I see when I turn out the light?" and, as it was 1967, McCartney managed a drug reference, "I get high...". Ringo learned his lines in the studio, refusing to sing just one couplet, "What would you do if I sang out of tune / Would you stand up and throw a tomato at me?" McCartney sensibly gave it an on-spot rewrite.

It wasn't the brightest buckle in *Sgt Pepper*'s dazzling, candy-coloured wardrobe, but, a year later, Joe Cocker was on the toilet in the back yard of his Sheffield home, humming the track to himself, as you do. This, according to the windmill-armed singer, was where he had the eureka moment that gave him his career break. Instead of walking-blues, however, Cocker was thinking in 3/4 time. At rehearsals he suggested to his group, the Grease Band, that they play the song as a waltz, telling his organist, Tommy Eyre, to "change the chords in the verse to make it more classical". For the Olympic studios session, the soon-to-be Led Zeppelin guitarist Jimmy Page and drummer B.J. Wilson were drafted in.

After 13 takes, they'd nailed it: "You just know when you go into the control room," recalled Eyre. "It doesn't matter who's on the mixing desk – it's like God's taken over." Ringo's likeable singalong was transformed into gut-wrenching soul. The Beatles loved it and sent Cocker a telegram, reading "Thanks – you are far too much". Subsequent covers followed, notably a Nineties take by soppy popsters Wet Wet Wet, which most rushed to forget. "It's been picked up and used a lot, that song," said McCartney. "I think that was probably the best of the songs we wrote for Ringo, actually."

CARAVAN OF LOVE
THE HOUSEMARTINS (1986)
Original by Isley, Jasper, Isley (1983)

No one was more thrilled than Chris Jasper when the Housemartins – four clean-cut kids from the English port of Hull – took 'Caravan of Love' to Number One at Christmas 1986.

In 1973, the Isley Brothers vocal trio expanded to embrace Jasper, a brother-in-law, and two younger siblings, the guitarist Ernie Isley and the bass-playing Marvin Isley. A decade on, with a succession of modern soul classics behind them, the family split. Jasper, who'd become the group's foremost arranger and songwriter, teamed up with Ernie and Marvin to form a new vocal threesome, with a typically Eighties name that makes them sound like a firm of corporate attorneys: Isley, Jasper, Isley.

Their enchanting hit, 'Caravan of Love', follows in the tracks of the O'Jays' 'Love Train': an appeal for all-comers to jump aboard and unite in global amity. "I had been looking at the world scene quite a bit," said Jasper. "I wasn't pleased with what I was seeing." Jasper's message of hope was written around a tune he been humming for a month. Sitting with a blank notepad one afternoon, Jasper began scribbling his thoughts. After just 20 minutes, he clicked his Biro. The song was finished. It wasn't exactly William Blake, but tethered to the exquisite melody that had been bugging Jasper for weeks, the song glides in on a positive note that is both assured and inspiring.

'Caravan of Love' was recorded at a studio in East Orange, New Jersey, as the title track to their second album, with Jasper taking keyboard and lead vocal duties and Ernie and Marvin on everything else, including no less than two synthesisers. Jasper described listening to the playbacks as like hearing a film score unfold. It languished on America's R&B charts for a full six months, until the four white boys from Hull picked it up and made it part of their live *a cappella* act. Isley, Jasper, Isley could not repeat the success, however, and the partnership dissolved in the late Eighties. Falling short in securing a lasting world peace, the song has since been used, with perhaps ironic inevitability, to advertise Dodge Caravans on American television.

I'M A BELIEVER
ROBERT WYATT (1974)
Original by the Monkees (1967)

In 1974, Robert Wyatt, the former drummer with earnest prog-jazzers Soft Machine, reminded us of what a great song 'I'm a Believer' is, returning it to the Top 20 in a droll version which cast the wheelchair-bound Marxist with a voice like Marmite as the most unlikely of pop stars.

The song itself was, of course, a huge hit for the Monkees and was penned by Neil Diamond, in the days when Diamond was a jobbing writer. "Fifth Monkee" might lack the cachet of "fifth Beatle", or even "sixth Stone", but by the middle of 1967, that's what the papers were calling Diamond. The songwriter had produced two of the Monkees' first three singles and was fast becoming a one-man hit machine. Bill Wexler, Diamond's keyboard player, recalled him clowning around with an acoustic guitar, singing a new composition in late 1966, in the deep drawl he used on his own recordings. Diamond's original idea was to have 'I'm a Believer' recorded by a country artist. He even had a singer in mind, Eddy Arnold, the country superstar, who'd bounced all over the charts in 1965 with 'Make the World Go Away'.

But Don Kirshner changed all that. The New York music publisher was scouting for talent: tunesmiths who could write for his latest project, the Monkees. Billed as "America's answer to the Beatles", and with a knockabout television series inspired by the film *A Hard Day's Night*, the manufactured group was the successful creation of two producers from Screen Gems-Columbia, Bob Rafelson and Bert Schneider. It was Kirshner's job to hustle up some hits. After the first single, 'Last Train to Clarksville', topped the charts, Kirshner ran his finger through his phone book and it settled on Diamond. "I told him… there was a song I had just completed that I liked very much," recalled Diamond, "I went over and played it for him." Kirshner negotiated for the song, insisting that the songwriter relinquish the publishing rights to Screen Gems. With thoughts of Eddy Arnold dwindling in his mind, Diamond agreed.

The backing track, onto which the Monkees' vocals would be overdubbed, was produced by Jeff Barry. He used Diamond's regular musicians and the writer provided a guide vocal. There was trouble when Mike Nesmith of the Monkees first heard it. "He said 'that ain't no hit', and it got real embarrassing," recalled Barry. Eventually, Nesmith was ejected from the recording studio and Mickey Dolenz cut the lead vocal. The release confirmed the Monkees' position as the TV/pop phenomenon of 1967. Diamond recorded his own string-laden rendition in 1971, but Wyatt's is the version of choice.

DIRTY OLD TOWN
THE POGUES (1985)
Original by Ewan MacColl (1950)

For a man who disliked American-inflected pop, Ewan MacColl wrote some matchless international chart hits. 'The First Time Ever I Saw Your Face', covered by the Chicago soulstress Roberta Flack is as graceful as any love ballad from the American songbook. Conversely, 'Dirty Old Town', taken to a new generation by the Pogues in the mid Eighties, is smudged with postwar England's blackened smokestacks and back-to-backs. In fact, it was Salford, Lancashire, where MacColl was born plain Jimmy Miller (the name change came in the mid Fifties). After WWII he co-founded a socialist drama project, Theatre Workshop, with his first wife, the radical theatre innovator, Joan Littlewood. Their documentary play about the railway town, 'Landscape With Chimneys', braved the boards in 1950.

On the opening night, Littlewood, hit a problem. An awkward scene change required something to keep the audience's attention for a couple of minutes. MacColl's hands reached for his guitar and his mind drifted through the theatre doors to the sooted streets. His father, unemployed for long periods in the Thirties, would spend time at the Workers' Arts Club, in the town's Liverpool Street. "Next to it was a cinder croft, and behind that the main gasworks for Salford," MacColl said. The memory pricked his imagination. MacColl quickly marshalled the images into a somber folk tune that got its first performance two hours later.

The song is built on Salford's smoke-encrusted brick. "I have absorbed this place through the palms of my hands," MacColl wrote. "Of course I hate it, I loathe it, I am scared of being devoured by it; and yet, though I live to be a hundred, it is unlikely that I will ever come to know any place as well as I know this one." MacColl claims he had forgotten the song until he learned, to his apparent alarm, that it was being sung by American folk revivalists. It has since been covered by numerous artists, including Rod Stewart. For the Pogues' raucous, booze-soaked rendition, included on their second album, *Rum Sodomy & the Lash*, Shane MacGowan sings the song as viewed through the bottom of a whiskey glass. Ian Campbell, who cut a version in 1966, detected in it "a quality which tends to make it sound like the background music for an old Western": it was MacColl's unwitting riposte to Americana.

FOR ONCE IN MY LIFE
STEVIE WONDER (1968)
Original by Jean DuShon (1966)

Generally thought of these days as a Stevie Wonder original, 'For Once in my Life' wasn't always his. It was written by Orlando Murden and lyricist Ronald Miller and was first recorded by a Detroit jazz vocalist called Jean DuShon. She'd started out in 1961, with Phil Spector and a tune called 'Talk to Me', made a few more 45s and in 1966 was scouting for new material. Miller caught one of her concerts and invited her over. "Ron came and was so excited over my sound and he said 'Jean, I have a tune for you and I know that you can do it'," she recalled. DuShon gave the song a read-through and Miller liked it so much he took her round to Chess studios.

DuShon's prototype of 'For Once in my Life' was released on Cadet, a Chess subsidiary, and was soon record of the week at Detroit's WXYZ Radio. The song gained a reputation and DuShon was poised for a breakthrough. But sales suffered from poor promotion: there was even a rumour that the release was spiked by Tamla Motown's founding father, Berry Gordy, who – as Miller was under contract to Motown – wanted it for his own. Tony Bennett grazed the charts with a leisurely version late in 1967, but the song was about to get a makeover. Gordy had found the right singer for the song: his teenage prodigy, Stevie Wonder, whose career was on the rise with the finger-popping 'Uptight' and 'I Was Made to Love Her'.

Wonder and his producer, Hank Cosby, jumped on 'For Once in my Life'. They sped it up, gave it a string arrangement, complete with an animated piccolo motif, and turned it into his biggest hit to date, kept from the US Number One spot only by his fellow Motowner, Marvin Gaye. Wonder's probable lack of enthusiasm at singing someone else's song is more than concealed by his exuberant performance. Scores of successful covers followed, all to DuShon's chagrin. A big-band version by Frank Sinatra in 1969 was the final straw. "Before I knew it everybody else was jumping on it," DuShon said. The disappointment dogged her for years. With a poignant nod at the song's lyrics, she eventually let it go: "I stopped singing it, it wasn't mine anymore."

GLORIA
PATTI SMITH (1975)
Original by Them (1964)

Patti Smith wasn't especially interested in 'Gloria', Van Morrison's smouldering tale of lust from his days with the Belfast five-piece, Them. She was simply selecting three-chord songs that could be used as a framework for her spontaneous verse. "I liked the rhythm, and we just sort of used it for our own design," she said. The formula worked better than she could have imagined. Richard Sohl's soft, Debussy-like piano and Lenny Kaye's pungent guitar accompany the most memorable of openers: "Jesus died for somebody's sins, but not mine", a line resurrected from her 1971 poem, 'Oath'. Smith described it as her youthful manifesto on freedom: "I wasn't saying that I didn't like Christ... just that I wanted to take the responsibility for the things I do."

It's the song that, Morrison once said, sounds best played live for 20 minutes. His own concert recording, on the 1974 set, *It's Too Late To Stop Now*, runs to a disappointingly short three-and-a-bit minutes. Smith stretches it to fit her own lyrics, mixing in her poetry and adjusting the tempo accordingly, from canter to gallop.

'Gloria' was written in 1964, as a tribute to a close cousin of Morrison's, Gloria Gordon, who had recently died of cancer: "I dug her", the singer has said of his muse. It first appeared as the B-side to the Them single 'Baby Please Don't Go', the famous triple-chord riff supplied by their guitarist, Billy Harrison (who was shortchanged in the writing credits).

By the mid Sixties it was on the set-lists of most American garage-bands. When Jim Morrison and the Doors wrapped-up their summer season at Hollywood's Whisky-A-Go-Go in 1966, Them were also on the bill. "We all got pretty soused and we ended up all getting on stage together and playing

'Gloria'," recalled the Doors' Robby Krieger. There are blurred photographs of the two tousle-haired Morrisons jamming together, but apparently no-one thought to tape it. Smith idolised Jim Morrison and knew 'Gloria' well enough. She gave her version a subtitle, 'In Excelsis Deo', and made it the first track on *Horses*, her influential and iconic debut album from 1975. Van Morrison approved: "If something comes along like what Patti Smith is doing, I have a tendency now to accept it as what it is and I get off".

AIN'T NO SUNSHINE
MICHAEL JACKSON (1971)
Original by Bill Withers (1971)

Michael Jackson's 'Ain't No Sunshine' didn't even make it to 45 in the United States. It was the original, by Bill Withers, which gained the airplay and Billboard chart success. In the UK Jackson's cover was the third single taken from his debut solo, 1971's *Got To Be There* (and is the opening track to the album). It breezed into the charts in the summer of 1972 where it seemed to linger like an August sunset.

Meanwhile Withers was enjoying contemporaneous UK chart action with a different song, 'Lean On Me'. At 32, Withers, originally from rural Slab Fork, West Virginia, was something of a latecomer. He had spent nine years in the US Navy, where he underwent speech therapy to overcome a stuttering problem, before taking a job installing lavatories on Boeing 747s. In 1970 he signed with the Hollywood independent Sussex Records and set about recording his first album. On paper, he seemed an unlikely prospect for chart action. On vinyl, his strategy of "simple yet sophisticated" couldn't fail. "Simple is memorable," said Withers. "If something's too complicated, you're not going to walk around humming it to yourself because it's too hard to remember. It's very difficult to make things simple and understandable."

It had been a long road to the studio. His early demo bounced around various labels in the late Sixties, until it reached the ears of the Stax keyboard player and producer, Booker T. Jones. Jones saw the potential and brought in some top-drawer musicians, including Al Jackson and Donald Dunn from his band, The MGs, plus the guitarist Stephen Stills. Together they cut what would become Withers' debut, *Just As I Am*. The launch single was a pounding summer anthem, 'Harlem'. It didn't quite hit the hot spot, however, so DJs flipped the record and instead pushed the laid-back, bare-boned soul of 'Ain't No Sunshine'.

Its title was perhaps borrowed from Norman Whitfield's 1967 Motown classic, 'Ain't No Sun Since You've Been Gone'. Withers' trademark hook, however, is a repetitive ad-lib, "I know, I know, I know", which enabled him to show off his breath-control as a singer. "I wasn't going to do that," he said. "I was going to write something there". But Jones told him to keep it in and Withers felt he ought to comply. "They were all these people with all this experience and all these reputations, and I was this factory worker just sort of puttering around." The song won a Grammy for best R&B song in 1971, and lives on: in 1991 Paul McCartney released an unplugged live version and in 2001 it was sampled by the rapper DMX, for his song 'No Sunshine'.

BLACKWATER SIDE
LED ZEPPELIN (1969)
Original arrangement by Anne Briggs (1963)

'Black Mountain Side', the instrumental interlude on Led Zeppelin's first album, passed through many hands on its way to one of Rock's most powerful debuts. Zeppelin's guitarist, Jimmy Page, claims he first heard 'Blackwater Side', a traditional Irish number, from Anne Briggs in a London club. Briggs, the Nottingham folk singer with a voice as fine as a lacewing, had made the song her own in 1963. It was brought to her attention by the folk collector, Bert Lloyd, who exhumed a field recording of it from the BBC archives. The raw, unaccompanied version Briggs heard was by 21-year-old Mary Doran, part of a group of Travellers found singing around a campfire on the outskirts of Belfast in 1952 and captured for posterity by Peter Kennedy of the English Folk Dance and Song Society.

The ballad of how a young man spied a "lovely maid" in a shady grove was first published in the 1880s, by the broadside printer Henry Such. Here, the man seduces the girl and proves himself an honourable lover. "It's one of those pieces whose verses have floated in from half-a-dozen other songs," commented Lloyd. By the time it reached Briggs, it had become a familiar tale of broken promises. She arranged it for the guitar, borrowing her accompaniment from another folk comrade, Stan Ellison. If Briggs was the catalyst in the popularisation of 'Blackwater Side', then her musical partner in the early Sixties, Bert Jansch, was its champion: "I remember learning [it] from Anne, basically by playing on the guitar exactly what she'd sung and then fitting riffs to it," said Jansch.

His baroque arrangement became a cornerstone of the seminal 1966 album, *Jack Orion*, and inspired Page's arrangement. When Jansch heard 'Black Mountain Side', credited to Page and augmented with a tabla drum, to give it an Eastern flavour, a half-cocked legal case ensued, eventually abandoned when Jansch could not of course prove the song was his. In truth, 'Blackwater Side' belongs to no-one, although it has been coveted by many, from Sandy Denny and Linda Thompson to the Celtic folk-rockers Altan. All have Briggs to thank. "I don't personally identify with the sentiments," she said. "But it's a lovely thing to sing and, in the midst of the swinging Sixties, was a sad reminder of a harsher and unequal sexual morality that still lingers on."

FELL IN LOVE WITH A BOY
JOSS STONE (2003)
Original by the White Stripes (2001)

At first listen, 'Fell in Love with a Girl', the White Stripes second UK and first US hit in the spring of 2002, from their *White Blood Cells* album, doesn't exactly lend itself to a smoky soul cover. But Joss Stone's radical rework of Jack White's dogeared modern love story, retitled 'Fell in Love with a Boy', faithfully follows Rule One of covering songs – do it different. The White Stripes' song is a two-minute, thunderous salvo of guitar and clattering percussion and produced to sound like White was still working the song out whilst it was being recorded (at Easley Studio in Memphis, Tennessee, with ersatz sister Meg on backing vocals, as well as drums).

The central hook bears some resemblance to the guitar solo in Tom Petty's 1993 single 'Mary Jane's Last Dance', but no matter – it's a terrific blast of modern-day garage punk that would have probably changed the world had it have been released in 1976. As it is, *Rolling Stone* magazine ranked in as one of the Top 40 songs that altered the course of pop history.

It was unavoidable in the summer of 2001, when Joss Stone was a still a schoolgirl. No doubt she had early designs on the song. Backed by singers Angie Stone and Betty Wright, the 16-year-old Stone turns the lights down low and tidies away any sharp objects. The track, recorded in Philadelphia, was an unexpected last-minute inclusion on her 2003 soul covers album, *The Soul Sessions*, alongside vintage material from the likes of Sugar Billy, the Isley Brothers and Carla Thomas. Stone sings it like she believes it and the track was generally well received – except by hardcore White Stripes fans. White, however, ever the musical adventurer, approved heartily and even pastiched it in a slower version when the White Stripes played it live. "How's that for approval," said Stone. "Cool bloke, Jack White!"

MONY MONY
BILLY IDOL (1981)
*Original by Tommy James and the Shondells
(1968)*

In July 1981 the former Generation X vocalist, Billy Idol, stood in LA's Musicland West studio and curled his snarling lip around a brainless lyric. Perhaps not the most demanding number in the popular songbook, 'Mony Mony' was an odd choice to cover for the one-time London punk but it swiftly became a live favourite and when he released a concert version in 1987 it shot into the Top 10. By then 'Mony Mony' was 20 years old.

Back in 1968 Tommy James had a song, but no title. He couldn't have 'Bonie Maronie', but it needed to be something like that. "We were going through the dictionary but nothing was happening," said James. Frustrated, he stepped onto the terrace of his Manhattan apartment for some air and gazed out at the forest of high-rises. His eye caught a flashing neon sign atop the 40-storey Mutual Of New York insurance building, on Broadway. "All of a sudden, here's this M.O.N.Y., with a dollar sign in the middle of the O," he said. The title was right there. He called his writing partner, Richie Cordell, over to the terrace: "We both fell down laughing."

James finished off the song, complete with title hook, and went to Allegro studio, on Broadway, just down from the Mutual Of New York. The basement recording facility, above a subway tunnel, had a superb live feel and was where James, as well as vocal groups like the Four Seasons, had made earlier hits. His band was a five-strong garage outfit that included the guitarist Mick Jones, pianist Ronnie Rosman and Peter Lucia on drums. The Shondells shuffled for floorspace, the monitors flickered to life and they started up a ruckus that drowned out the subway's muffled rumble. Released in 1968, on Major

Minor in the UK, 'Mony Mony' quickly climbed to Number One. The pounding call-and-response climaxes with a high-octane energy: it was a huge party hit.

The year after Idol's cover, 'I Think We're Alone Now', one of James's best efforts, was a hit in the hands of the teenage Tiffany. In more recent years Status Quo returned 'Mony Mony' to the charts.

After his chart success, James showed he was anything but brainless, by heading out on the campaign trail with the Democratic presidential candidate, Hubert Humphrey, who later repaid the effort by providing liner notes for a Shondells album. In 1970, after a few follow-up hits, such as the more whimsical 'Crimson and Clover', James and the Shondells went their separate ways.

THIS WHEEL'S ON FIRE
SIOUXSIE AND THE BANSHEES (1987)
Original by Julie Driscoll, Brian Auger and the Trinity (1968)

It seems perhaps only natural that Siouxsie and the Banshees should have got around to recording 'This Wheel's On Fire'. As Mod's first lady, Julie Driscoll was, after all, an unwitting influence on the class of '76. When the Banshees began assembling their album of covers, *Through The Looking Glass* – which included gothed-up versions of Sparks' 'This Town Ain't Big Enough for the Both of Us' and Television's 'Little Johnny Jewel' – the old Driscoll number must have seemed an obvious choice.

Back in the mid Sixties Driscoll was a shimmering muse in a space-age hairstyle and vinyl-black eyeliner. In 1965 she was working for Giorgio Gomelsky, who managed the Yardbirds, opening the post, typing up letters and trying to keep her fledgling singing career going. She met Brian Auger, a jazz and blues organist, when he was called in to play on one of her early singles. Auger was impressed and Driscoll leapt at the invitation to join his R&B assembly, Steampacket, which also featured a lean young vocalist named Rod Stewart. When the packet ran out of steam, Auger and his bassist and drummer became the Trinity, and Driscoll their iconic frontwoman. In early 1968, Gomelsky played Auger and Driscoll a tape of some unreleased songs by Bob Dylan. Manfred Mann had already bagged 'Mighty Quinn', but 'This Wheel's on Fire' was up for grabs.

The song has its origins in the fabled "Basement Tapes", which Dylan recorded in 1967, with The Band, in the cellar of a pink, clapboard house they'd rented in upstate New York. Dylan brought in some lyrics about a wheel rolling down the road, for which The Band's Rick Danko found a suitable melody.

It may have been Dylan coming to terms with his near-fatal motorcycle accident in 1966, which kept him from the public eye for over a year. Driscoll and Trinity's definitive cover was released in the spring of 1968 and made the Top Five. "We went through the star trip and peoples' heads went through the ozone," Auger, said. Meanwhile, in January of the same year, The Band had cut a phased version, for their debut album, *Music From Big Pink*.

Dylan's original didn't officially make it up from the basement until Columbia released the much-bootlegged tapes in 1975. By then Driscoll and Trinity were a fading pop memory and 'This Wheel's on Fire' little more than a Sixties curio. By the Nineties it was precisely this quality that attracted the comedienne, Jennifer Saunders, who was writing a new BBC sitcom with a retro-feel, *Absolutely Fabulous*. The wheel turned full spin and Driscoll was coaxed back into the studio to re-record the song as the show's theme.

BETTE DAVIS EYES
KIM CARNES (1981)
Original by Jackie DeShannon (1974)

Kim Carnes was in the studio recording 'Bette Davis Eyes' as news of the shooting of John Lennon began filtering through New York City, that night in December 1980. Shocked and in disbelief, Carnes pressed on and cut her track live, over three takes, the following day.

The song almost never made it. Its composer, Kentucky-born Jackie DeShannon, was one of early rock 'n' roll's rare female all-rounders. She penned hits for the Searchers and Brenda Lee, co-wrote with a very junior Randy Newman, and sessioned on Jimmy Page's first solo single in 1964. In 1974, DeShannon was working on material for her own album, *New Arrangement*, with a fellow songwriter, Donna Weiss. "[Weiss] brought in a big stack of lyrics," said DeShannon. "She said she couldn't get anyone to help her with it and could I take a look." DeShannon, inspired by the film *Now Voyager*, and in particular the scene in which Paul Henreid lights cigarettes for Bette Davis, worked out a melody for a song which name-checked Hollywood heroines.

DeShannon demoed 'Bette Davis Eyes' as a straight-ahead rocker, but for the album, it was recorded as a schmaltzy jazz-shuffle, much to DeShannon's disappointment. "The producer and I really had a lot of disagreements... It was not the rock version we gave him," she said. When the album flopped, 'Bette Davis Eyes' was written off by DeShannon as a lost opportunity. Five years later, Weiss was visiting her friend Kim Carnes and had with her a tape of some songs she thought Carnes might like. Included was the original demo of 'Bette Davis Eyes'. Carnes, who had enjoyed a career singing with Kenny Rogers and writing songs for Frank Sinatra and David Cassidy, heard her future.

She loved 'Bette Davis Eyes', but it needed a new hook to take it into the Eighties. Her keyboard player, Bill Cuomo, wrote a synthesiser riff to give it the necessary contemporary feel. Carnes knew she had a hit. DeShannon was both surprised and delighted at Carnes' husky arrangement: "Her voice was perfect for it," she said. Carnes, DeShannon and Weiss all claimed Grammys for their part in its eventual success. And what did Bette Davis make of it? "After the release of the record, Miss Davis sent me a note explaining how much she loved the song," said Carnes, who performed it in front of the movie legend at a tribute concert, just before Davis died in 1989.

COMFORTABLY NUMB
SCISSOR SISTERS (2004)
Original by Pink Floyd (1979)

"I've been singing it for the latter half of my life," said Scissor Sisters' Jake Shears of the 1979 Pink Floyd classic, 'Comfortably Numb'. Shears recorded his falsetto tribute with Scissor Sisters in 2003, turning it into a huge chart hit the following year, much to the annoyance of most Floyd fans. They weren't the first to take Pink Floyd to the discotheque, however. Thirty years earlier, *Discoballs*, by Rosebud, a studio group comprising French off-duty prog-rockers, provided a novel approach to the Floyd back catalogue, all at a 4/4 beat. In 1977, the year *Discoballs* rolled across European dance-floors, Pink Floyd's bassist, Roger Waters, fell ill before a gig in Philadelphia. A doctor diagnosed possible food poisoning. "He wasn't listening to me at all," Waters told *Rolling Stone*. "I discovered later on that I had hepatitis."

A tranquilizer was administered and Waters persuaded to go on stage. "Boy, that was the longest two hours of my life," he said. After the injection, Waters could barely move his limbs. "God knows what he gave me, but it was some very heavy muscle relaxant." Waters scribbled some lines based on his experience. Terrifying and claustrophobic, 'Comfortably Numb' confirmed Waters as one of the best lyricists of the period. His words suited a remnant melody which Pink Floyd's guitarist, David Gilmour, had left over from the recording of his first solo album. But in the studio the pair couldn't agree on which direction to take 'Comfortably Numb'. Gilmour wanted heavy rock 'n' roll. Waters argued for a slower, orchestral arrangement. "We argued over 'Comfortably Numb' like mad," said Gilmour.

Eventually they opted for a quiet opening and used Gilmour's blistering, iconic solos to end the song. It was a staple of Pink Floyd concerts, closing their appearance at Live8 in 2005, and has also been performed by both Waters and Gilmour separately – and perhaps more surprisingly by Van Morrison, for the 2006 Leonardo DiCaprio movie, *The Departed*. There have been country and chillout versions, string quartet and reggae interpretations. Gilmour applauded the Scissor Sisters' cover, although a planned duet between him and Shears at New York's Radio City Music Hall was called off at the eleventh hour. "I'm emotionally fragile and weeping," said Shears at the cancellation. "I was so over the moon because I can sing the hell out of that song."

FREAK LIKE ME
SUGABABES (2002)
Original by Adina Howard (1995)

Sugababes (2002 lineup: Heidi Range, Keisha Buchanan and Mutya Buena) first heard 'Freak Like Me' as preteens in 1995, when it was a low-30s UK hit for the R&B singer Adina Howard. Howard's version is itself barely original: Sly Stone samples nestle in the mix and the melody rests heavily on a mid-paced funk cut from 1976 called 'I'd Rather Be With You', by Bootsy Collins and George Clinton (subsequently credited as co-writers of 'Freak Like Me'). The single had a fan in Richard X, though. In 2001 the producer made his name with a series of white-label bootlegs, released under the name Girls On Top. One, dubbed 'We Don't Give A Damn About Our Friends', adeptly grafted Howard's a cappella vocals onto an "interpolation", as he put it, of Gary Numan's 1979 debut, 'Are "Friends" Electric'. It became a club anthem and commercial release beckoned.

A slightly bemused Numan was happy to grant permission. Howard, however, declined. Richard X needed someone else to re-cut the vocals. Sugababes, newly signed to Island Records, weren't too familiar with Bootsy Collins, and even less Numan. "I didn't have a clue who Gary Numan was," said Buchanan. "I wasn't born until 1984. But my parents told me about him." No matter: they loved Richard X's mash-up. "We tried it out and everyone was like, that's the first single!" said Buena. Island pressed up a limited 'Are Freaks Electric' on vinyl, credited to Girls On Top Vs Sugababes, before remixing it for the charts. The rougher edges of Richard X's original were sensibly left untouched. "The one that was released ended up using my same loops," he said. "Apart from the Sugababes singing it, it was almost the same seven-inch that I'd put out."

It zones in on a spacey sound effect, lifted from an Eighties video game, and segues neatly into Numan's electro classic. In spring 2002 it made Number One, reviving the trio's flagging career and becoming one of the decade's defining records, bringing the mash-up into the mainstream. It now features on the crucial genre compilation *Richard X Presents His X Factor, Vol. 1*. "Sometimes people don't think you can mix two songs together and make it sound good," reckoned Buena. "But in general I think it's really good to mix an Eighties [sic] track and a 94 [sic] track together."

Robert Webb

HANGING ON THE TELEPHONE
BLONDIE (1978)
Original by the Nerves (1976)

Stuck on punk's West Coast outpost, the Nerves' fame barely made it out of California. The trio recorded a solitary, self titled, EP of spiky power-pop in 1976 before collapsing in a tangle of skinny ties and pencil-tight trousers. By the summer of 1978 their sound had been appropriated by other likeminded Los Angeles outfits such as the Knack and their primary songwriter, Jack Lee, was facing financial ruin. One song on the Nerves' EP, however, was about to change his fortunes. "I remember the day vividly," Lee told *Mojo* magazine in 2007. "It was a Friday. They were going to cut off our electricity at six o'clock, the phone too."

Before his services were disconnected, the phone rang. Debbie Harry was on the line telling Lee, "We really like your song 'Hanging on the Telephone' and we want to record it on our album." Blondie had shared a bill with the Nerves during their first trip west and Harry and the band picked up on the song, which was inspired partly by an image Lee had seen by Beatles illustrator Alan Aldridge and partly by his girlfriend. Most memorably, it kicked off with a telephone dialling tone (a trick shortly to be used by ELO on their hit 'Telephone Line'). Blondie rehearsed it before convening to record their third album, the career defining *Parallel Lines*, produced by Mike Chapman, the man who had kicked glam up the charts with Mud and Suzi Quatro. "That track was magic from the beginning," said Chapman, who urged the band to play it in the studio as though they were performing to a live audience.

'Hanging on the Telephone' was a throwback to Blondie's earlier, rough-edged sound. They ran through four takes – with Harry's lacerating vocals and Clem Burke's bayonet drumming driving the song – and Chapman selected the most energetic to polish up as the album's opener. Crucially, a telephone sound effect – although Chapman chose a British ring tone – was kept as the opener. The song made the Top Five in November 1978 and has subsequently been covered by many, including Girls Aloud and Def Leppard. Lee, who went on to pen 'Come Back and Stay' for Paul Young, regretted his own version was never a hit, although he claims he always knew 'Hanging on the Telephone' was a special song: "Even people who hated me – and there were plenty – had to admit it was great."

HAZY SHADE OF WINTER
THE BANGLES (1987)
Original by Simon and Garfunkel (1966)

In 1982 Susanna Hoffs was juggling her role fronting the Bangles with a day job in a ceramics factory. Her only company was the oldies station on the radio. "It was very lonely in this room, all by myself, all day," said Hoffs. One morning Simon and Garfunkel's 'A Hazy Shade of Winter' crackled across the factory floor. Written by Paul Simon during his sojourn in England and issued as a single in 1966, it was, by the Eighties, better known as a track on the 1968 album *Bookends*. "When I heard that song, I thought, that's so perfect for the Bangles," said Hoffs, who began including it in her band's live sets.

Fast forward to 1987, when Hoffs was asked to come up with material for the soundtrack to Marek Kanievska's movie *Less than Zero*. 'Hazy Shade of Winter' (the Bangles dispensed with the indefinite article), a chilly view of how time crushes youth, fit the bill perfectly. Simon's austere opening bars, delivered in the original version on a tambourine and acoustic guitar, were converted by the producer Rick Rubin into a bludgeoning, steam-hammer riff. The band rattled through their cover, omitting the final verse altogether. It was issued as a single on Rubin's Def Jam label and, unexpectedly, charted. "We were all so surprised that it did so well," said the Bangles' bassist, Michael Steele.

Simon had hitherto dismissed the original single, along with others he cut with Art Garfunkel in the mid Sixties: "They didn't mean a lot. They weren't well recorded," he said. When he heard the Bangles take on his song, he was uncharacteristically complimentary: "That happens to be a really nice cover," he said. "It's unusual that a cover can be as good as the original. I think that's maybe better than the original." The ultimate tribute came in 2003, when Simon and

Garfunkel reunited for the *Old Friends* concert and rearranged 'A Hazy Shade of Winter' from the Bangles' cover. Hoffs met with Simon after their single was a hit. "I don't think we talked about it very much," she said. "I remember he was very sweet, and I'm sure he was happy the song had done so well." It has also been covered by Bob Dylan and eventually charted in the UK for Simon and Garfunkel in 1991.

HURT
JOHNNY CASH (2002)
Original by Nine Inch Nails (1994)

"If you're not ready for it, it's terrible, it's noise," Trent Reznor told one newspaper, on the release of the 1994 Nine Inch Nails album, *The Downward Spiral*. The nihilistic concept album about addiction, also known as *Halo 8* and the third release from the industrial rock outfit fronted by Reznor, is a fathomless chasm which bottoms out into a painful, stomach-tightening ballad called 'Hurt'. "By the end of that record, everything's been discarded, and things that I'd looked for hope in have failed me," said Reznor. "['Hurt'] offers redemption through the desire for it." The album's final track examines how the drugs really don't work.

Initially, Reznor had doubts about including the song on the album. "[It's] based on the most personal sentiments, the deepest emotions I have ever had," he said. "We were crying when we made it, it was so intense." 'Hurt' was composed on the piano at Reznor's house in Beverly Hills, once the home of the actress Sharon Tate and the scene of her murder by the followers of Charles Manson in 1969. The walls of the room Reznor used for recording the song still bore the word "Pig" daubed in blood by Manson's acolytes, and so Reznor named the house Le Pig. After *The Downward Spiral* was completed, he had the building demolished, appalled at the thought he might have contributed to the Manson myth.

'Hurt' came to the attention of the country legend Johnny Cash in 2002, through a mutual friend, the producer Rick Rubin. Cash listened to Reznor's song 100 times, hailing it as "the best anti-drug song I ever heard", before recording it for the Rubin-produced *American IV: The Man Comes Around*. Reznor was unsure at first that a Cash cover would be a good thing. "I listened to it, and it seemed incredibly strange and wrong to me to hear that voice with my song," he said. When Mark Romanek's poignant video for the song was released, however, Reznor was moved to tears. With Cash clearly fading fast, it seemed the powerful version would be his epitaph. "I never got to meet Johnny," said Reznor. "But I'm happy I contributed the way I did. It felt like a warm hug."

NEXT
SCOTT WALKER (1968)
Original by Jacques Brel (1964)

In 1961, the playwright and poet Eric Blau heard a concert recording by the Belgian singer Jacques Brel, then largely unknown to the English-speaking world. Brel's chansons of debauchery were spat out with a Gallic passion and his tender love songs soared in their poetry. Blau was captivated and his wife, the singer Elly Stone, urged him to translate some of the songs into English. Five years later, Blau was introduced to the songwriter Mort Shuman by an American producer, Nat Shapiro. In the midst of penning hits for the likes of Elvis Presley and the Drifters, Shuman had spent some time in Paris, where he also had stumbled across Brel, persuading the singer to let Shuman take his extraordinary songs back to America.

In New York, the pair collaborated on a musical, *Jacques Brel is Alive and Well and Living in Paris*, which debuted in 1968 and has since been revived several times in the twenty-first century. 'Next', translated by Blau and Shuman from Brel's 1964 song 'Au Suivant', was a cornerstone of the show. If not exactly word perfect, it retains the original melody and spirit and was approved by Brel. A young man describes how he exchanged his innocence for a dose of gonorrhoea at a mobile army whorehouse. The boys queue, stepping up as the "queer lieutenant" slaps their arses and barks the word that has haunted him since: "Next!". The black humour both shocked and titillated audiences around the world.

The pop star Scott Walker was already familiar with Brel when the show opened. "A German girl I knew at the time would play his records into the night," he said. "I just loved them." Walker mentioned Brel to Andrew Loog Oldham, the Rolling Stones' manager, who just happened to have been sent demos of Shuman and Blau's translations. "I asked if I could cover them," said Walker. Within a week he had set up a session: "It immediately unlocked my imagination". Walker's 'Next' was held over for his second solo album, 1968's *Scott 2*, produced by John Frantz. He went on to record many Brel songs during 1968 and 1969.

Marc Almond and Gavin Friday have also covered it and in 1973 Alex Harvey cut his own demonic version, dowsed in rock histrionics and Glasgow menace, for his album of the same name. Harvey's version may top Walker's, as he counts in the song's tango rhythm through clenched teeth: "N-E-X-T".

MIDNIGHT TRAIN TO GEORGIA
GLADYS KNIGHT AND THE PIPS (1973)
Original by Cissy Houston (1972)

Gladys Knight was beginning to feel like a second-class citizen at Motown, a label she had never wanted to sign with in the first place. During the boom years at Motor City she had been denied the house writing talents of Holland, Dozier and Holland and, despite a run of hits with the Pips, was an untended outpost in Berry Gordy's empire. After the appropriately valedictory 'Neither One of Us (Wants to be the First to Say Goodbye)', it was indeed farewell for Knight. As her Motown contract came up for renewal in 1973, she switched to the deliberately misspelled Buddah Records, established by the record executive Neil Bogart as a catch-all label for late-Sixties pop, rock and soul.

For Knight and the Pips it was a gamble that might not have paid off: their first single, 'Where Peaceful Waters Flow', created few ripples. But the second shunted all aside to top the charts. 'Midnight Train to Georgia' came from the prodigious writing talents of Jim Weatherly, who had given Knight 'Neither One of Us'. It was originally penned as a slow, Glen Campbell-style country number, 'Midnight Plane to Houston'. Weatherly had a phone conversation with the actress Farrah Fawcett. "We were just talking and she said she was packing," said Weatherly. "She was gonna take the midnight plane to Houston to visit her folks." He rang off and within the hour, the song was finished. Weatherly's original found its way, appropriately, to Cissy Houston, the mother of Whitney, who was signed to Atlantic. The coincidence in names would have sounded too gimmicky, so Atlantic switched Houston for Georgia and grounded Weatherly's night flight in favour of a rolling soul train.

Houston's cover of 'Midnight Train to Georgia' was a respectable hit in the US and Weatherly's publisher risked two bites at the cherry, forwarding the song to Knight. An instrumental backing (also used as the single's B-side) was recorded at the producer Tony Camillo's New Jersey studio and the Pips – Merald "Bubba" Knight, Eddie Patten and William Guest – cut their track in Detroit. "Some of the background vocals you hear on Gladys' records were first on Cissy Houston's record," claimed Weatherly. The hit, also the opener on the Pips' first post-Motown album, *Imagination*, earned Knight a Grammy for best R&B vocal group performance.

NOTHING COMPARES 2 U
SINÉAD O'CONNOR (1990)
Original by the Family (1985)

Not many careers have been launched with a tear. Sinéad O'Connor shot to Number One when her video for 'Nothing Compares 2 U' first aired on MTV at the dawn of the Nineties. As O'Connor sang, face to camera, her eyes welled. The lines she was singing had particular resonance for O'Connor, who as a child had suffered serious physical abuse at the hands of her mother. "It was an emotional thing for me," said O'Connor. "My mother was an extremely violent person," she said. "Someone who wasn't well." O'Connor's mother was killed in a car accident in the mid-Eighties. But by 1990, the abuse was still difficult for O'Connor to come to terms with. The video for 'Nothing Compares 2 U' was something of a cathartic experience for the Irish singer.

In tears of defiance, O'Connor converted one of Prince's half-forgotten cast-offs into the decade's first memorable chart topper. The song first appeared in 1985, as a track on *The Family*, the self-titled debut by a Paisley Park collective formed from the remnants of an earlier Prince band called The Time. Central to The Family was Prince's girlfriend at the time, Susannah Melvoin. With her in mind, the "Purple One" penned a love song, 'Nothing Compares 2 U'. Complete with a cathedral-like synthesiser and a piercing, Eighties-standard saxophone break, the track was recorded in the summer of 1984. The Family lacked Prince's full commitment however – the singer viewing the side project largely as a way of keeping Melvoin by his side. When the album finally appeared the following year, Prince had moved on to other things and no one took much notice of its sleeping giant.

Five years on, O'Connor gained a Grammy for her iconic cover – recorded, with the help of the producer Nellee Hooper, for her album *I Do Not Want What I Haven't Got* – and the opportunity to meet with the song's composer. She was duly invited to Prince's house in Los Angeles where, according to O'Connor, he berated her for using four-letter words in interviews. "When I told him to go fuck himself he got very upset and became quite threatening, physically," she said "I ended up having to escape." O'Connor made her getaway after parrying punches from the diminutive Prince. "All I could do was spit. I spat on him quite a bit."

Prince remained silent about the incident but, spurred by O'Connor's global hit with his song, subsequently included it in his live act, even releasing a live duet with Rosie Gaines, recorded on the Diamonds and Pearls tour in the early Nineties: a version with surpasses the original 1984 recording and, arguably, even O'Connor's cover. Prince had clearly warmed to the song after letting it languish in his back catalogue for several years, but O'Connor found it a difficult song to revisit: "I love it and I love singing it, but I'm afraid to sing it," she admitted.

Robert Webb

ONLY YOU
THE FLYING PICKETS (1983)
Original by Yazoo (1982)

It was the first UK a cappella Number One. More surprisingly, given that it was by six singers who had previously played a part in the miners' strikes of the Seventies, 'Only You' was, according to one source, prime minister Margaret Thatcher's favourite record of Christmas 1983.

If Flying Pickets were half-a-dozen once angry young men, then Yazoo were pop's odd couple. Vince Clarke bent over his synthesiser like a bleached pipe-cleaner with a floppy fringe. Alison Moyet, then known by the epithet Alf, was all smouldering eyeliner: larger than life and with a voice to match. Their musical interests collided in a techno-blues quite unlike any other in the early Eighties. Clarke was a founder member of Depeche Mode, whose hits 'New Life' and 'Just Can't Get Enough' helped put the independent label Mute Records on the mainstream map. Mute was formed in 1978 by Daniel Miller, initially to issue his own single, 'Warm Leatherette'. By specialising in electronic pop, the label soon carved a niche for itself. By far their biggest success in the Eighties was Depeche Mode.

After the band's debut album, *Speak and Spell*, Clarke fastened his synthesiser case and walked. "It would be out of order for me to say that their attitude was wrong. It was just different to mine," he said. Clarke palled up with Moyet after replying to an advert in the *Melody Maker*. Moyet, then aged 21, was searching for "rootsy blues musicians" to work with. Clarke wasn't quite that, but he had met the singer at a Saturday morning music school in their hometown of Basildon in the Seventies and liked her style. Back then, Moyet was learning the oboe and Clarke the violin. He gave her a call and Yazoo was born. Clarke played her 'Only You', which had been rejected by his former band for *Speak and Spell*. "I wanted to see it recorded," he said.

It turned out to be the perfect launch pad for the new partnership. Moyet sings a sad song through a rainy window, tugging at Clarke's baroque synthesiser arpeggio with real soul. It was produced by Clarke and Miller, with Eric Radcliffe, and issued on Mute in May 1982, reaching Number Two in the charts. A year later the Flying Pickets improved on its chart position in an imaginative arrangement. It has also been covered by Rita Coolidge and gained new appeal as the poignant background to the long-awaited final scene between Tim and Dawn in Ricky Gervais's sitcom *The Office*.

PIECE OF MY HEART
JANIS JOPLIN (1968)
Original by Erma Franklin (1967)

The proto-feminist soul-belter 'Piece of My Heart' was originally by Erma Franklin, Aretha's eldest, less fortunate, sister. Franklin began her career singing in church, with her sisters. In 1967, as Aretha's career was taking off at Atlantic, Erma signed up with Shout Records, run by the producer and songwriter Bert Berns, the author of 'Twist and Shout' and 'Here Comes the Night'. Berns gave Franklin her signature song, which he had written with his friend, Jerry Ragovoy. Before Franklin could capitalize on her success, however, things began falling apart. Just as she was about to embark on an album, Berns died suddenly of a heart attack. "It was utter chaos after that within the recording company," Franklin said. "So I got a job with a computer programming firm."

Her song passed to a gangly, white blues singer from Port Arthur, Texas. Janis Joplin recast the song in 1968, with her band of denimed hippy-rockers, Big Brother and the Holding Company. Her raw performance is captured on their second album, *Cheap Thrills*. "Come on, come on," Joplin urges, like no one had since the Beatles and "Please Please Me". It's a powerful holler and a far cry from Franklin's more restrained blueprint. When Franklin heard Joplin's cover on the radio, she claims she didn't even recognize the song. "Her version is so different from mine that I really don't resent it too much," she said. Franklin's career was hampered by misfortune. She quit the music industry in the Seventies and died in 2002.

The song has been covered by many other female vocalists, including Dusty Springfield, Beverley Knight and Bonnie Tyler, and even a few men – including a surprisingly soul-deep version by Deep Purple's former bassist Glenn Hughes, on a tribute album to Scottish band Nazareth, who cut their own hard rock version in 1989.

RAY OF LIGHT
MADONNA (1998)
Original by Curtiss Muldoon (1972)

Madonna wanted a record that sounded both "old and new at the same time". For the new she commissioned the producer and multi-instrumentalist William Orbit to revive the flagging Madonna brand. The old was partly provided by 'Sepheryn', a long-forgotten piece of progressive folk-rock whimsy by Dave Curtiss and Clive Maldoon. The succinctly named Curtiss Maldoon were an early signing to Deep Purple's vanity label, Purple – Curtiss had even narrowly missed fronting the hard rock pioneers in the late Sixties. 'Sepheryn' nestled on Curtiss Maldoon's self-titled debut, released in 1972. This sober strum around a lilting piano, with cryptic lyrics about a "ray of light", would have been less than a footnote in rock history, were it not for Maldoon's niece, Christine Leach.

In 1996, Leach, the singer with a trip-hop trio called Baby Fox, was recording in London with Orbit. They were listening to one of Orbit's backing tracks. "[It] fitted so well with the lyric to 'Sepheryn' that I just started singing it," said Leach. Keeping the first verse, she rewrote the chorus – "it was a kind of jam, really" – and firmed up the rather baggy melody. "It was excellent, and I said so," said Orbit. "I thought she'd written it, and she didn't say she hadn't." A few weeks later, the call from Madonna's record label partner, Guy Oseary, came through, conveying Madge's enthusiasm for Orbit's work. A tape, including the tracks recorded with Leach, was duly dispatched as the producer's calling card.

Madonna loved 'Sepheryn', describing it as "a mystical look at the universe and how small we are", and made further modifications, retitling it 'Ray of Light'. Recording got underway at Larrabee Studio, in Los Angeles, in the summer of 1997. Orbit produced and played most of the instruments.

"She must have loved the track," said Leach, when a copy of Madonna's take on her uncle's song reached her. "Even her ad libs are the same as mine." All five (Madonna, Orbit, Maldoon, Curtiss and Leach) were eventually credited as songwriters on what became a global hit in May 1998. Curtiss was initially annoyed at Madge's financial offer for "changing a couple of lines". "Then I realised that 15 per cent of millions is a lot better than 100 per cent of nothing," he said. "I did very well out of it."

SONG TO THE SIREN
THIS MORTAL COIL (1984)
Original by Tim Buckley (1967)

Tim Buckley's 'Song to the Siren' is something of a cult song. It was written by Buckley and Larry Beckett in 1967 and premiered in the most unlikely of places. Buckley, then the rising star of the new psychedelic folk-rock revolution was invited to appear on *The Monkees*, as Micky Dolenz's musical guest. It was the last ever episode of the children's TV show (in which the alt. fab four foil an evil mind-control plot), recorded in November 1967 and broadcast the following March. Buckley strides on with 12-string in hand and perches on the hood of a beat-up car. Rather than promoting new material, he picks out the delicate notes to an exquisite song which, at that point, was unrecorded.

It was a moving and unexpected performance, which can be seen in full on the DVD collection of rare Buckley performances, *My Fleeting House*. Beckett recalls how he wrote with Buckley. "I would write lyrics at my own inspiration, hand them to him and he would come back to me with a fully fledged piece," he says. "There was some kind of uncanny connection between us." 'Song to the Siren' remained the pair's favourite, right up until Buckley's death in 1974. "It's a perfect match of melody and lyrics," says Beckett. On vinyl, the song got off to a shaky start. After the performance on *The Monkees*, Buckley declined to include it on any of his subsequent three studio albums, instead handing it over to Pat Boone for *Departure*, Boone's 1969 collaboration with rock musicians. "Yo-ho-ho and bottle of rum!" chortles the clean-cut singer, amid the sound of screeching gulls, as he embarks on a listless croon.

It wasn't until 1970 that Buckley got around to the song again. With a few lyric changes, it was re-recorded for his album *Starsailor*. What turned it into a cult was a cover by This Mortal

Coil, for their 1984 album *It'll End in Tears*. Liz Frazer's ethereal vocals transformed the song into an unearthly hymn. Post-Coil, it has been covered by dozens, from Sally Oldfield to Robert Plant, some following Buckley's original, others imitating Frazer's distinctive phrasing. In a final twist to the story, Frazer began a romance with Buckley's son, Jeff, in the early Nineties.

THE LONG WAY HOME
NORAH JONES (2004)
Original by Tom Waits (2001)

'The Long Way Home' isn't the most obvious track on Norah Jones's sophomore set, *Feels Like Home*, but it has the best provenance. Tom Waits had sent Jones some demos of songs to suit her hushed, low-tar voice. Among them was this gentle number, penned by the gravel-throated Waits, with his wife, Kathleen Brennan. He waited for a reply, but heard nothing. "I met Tom and Kathleen at a concert he was doing," Jones explains on her website. "Tom asked me if I had listened to the demos he sent me." She hadn't but told Waits that, as a fan, she would make a point of finding them. When they turned up, Jones was bowled over. 'The Long Way Home' was the one, although at first Jones was reluctant to record it. She had already covered Waits in concert, but found it hard to better the originals.

Although Jones claims she hadn't heard the demo until pressed to do so by Waits, 'The Long Way Home' had actually been around for a couple of years, and she would have heard the song if she'd seen *Big Bad Love*, Arliss Howard's filmic take on the short stories of the Mississippi writer Larry Brown. Waits's own version first appeared, alongside tracks by Tom Verlaine and Steve Earle, on the bluesy soundtrack to this 2001 movie. On the original, recorded at Prairie Sun studios in Cotati, California, Waits exhales his lines like an air-brake, breathing a simple story of love and wanderlust.

Jones's version is similarly low-key. The walking-bass line ambles along like a worn-out mare, around a slow Johnny Cash figure-of-eight. There's food on the table and a roof overhead, but she'd trade it all for the highway if she could: "Money's just something you throw from the back of a train," as she sings, reading Waits to perfection. It was recorded in upstate New York, in April 2003, with the legendary producer Arif Mardin, who had done so much to launch Aretha Franklin's career in the Sixties. Mardin's R&B background was perfect for Jones: he'd already helped make her debut album a success. "She doesn't need pitch correction," he said of her singing on Feels Like Home. "She's always in tune and her voice always touches you."

VALERIE
AMY WINEHOUSE (2007)
Original by the Zutons (2006)

It has, in many ways, become Amy Winehouse's epitaph, so decisively did she make it her own. Sometimes it's easy to forget 'Valerie' wasn't always hers. Not to be confused with the hit of the same title by Steve Winwood, the Zutons' 'Valerie' was the song that gave the Liverpool band their breakthrough. It was, according to their lead singer, Dave McCabe, named for a friend he had met in America who had been caught drink-driving. The band's drummer, Sean Payne, has called it a "musical postcard to her, saying he's having a hard time and can she come over and see him." McCabe wrote it in a taxi on the way to visit his mother. "The whole song was written before I got there," said McCabe. "So 20 minutes, max." It was recorded at London's Townhouse Studios, with Stephen Street producing and the band playing together live. "The guitar arpeggio at the start was added as an afterthought to improve the intro," recalls Street. "It took a couple of attempts of mixing to get it right."

It was the second single taken from the band's album *Tired of Hanging Around*. A hit in the summer of 2006, it found an unlikely fan in Winehouse, who was still humming it a year later as she was invited to contribute to a new project with Mark Ronson. Winehouse, whom Ronson claimed only listened to things made before 1967, was struggling to come up with something that would fit the sessions for what would be Ronson's mega-selling album *Version*. "I explained that it was soul covers of guitar records," he said. Eventually Winehouse told Ronson that she might try 'Valerie'. Ronson strained to hear her voice singing it in his head. "I wasn't sure how it would work, but she went into the studio and tried it. I loved it," he said.

147

Ronson's production rested on a beat borrowed from the Jam's 'A Town Called Malice'. Winehouse also recorded a jazzier, acoustic version for Radio 1's *Live Lounge* which was issued at the same time as the Ronson collaboration and a hit in its own right, possibly due to download confusion – it was the Ronson version which got the airplay. The song has become something of a mixed blessing for McCabe. "I certainly have to try hard sometimes to not think about 'Valerie'," he said. "The days it's in my head are when I have to put down the guitar and just forget about writing."

LOUISIANA 1927
AARON NEVILLE (1991)
Original by Randy Newman (1974)

In 2005 Aaron Neville sang a vibrato version of Randy Newman's 'Louisiana 1927' for an NBC broadcast, *A Concert for Hurricane Relief*, in aid of the victims of Hurricane Katrina. It was a song he had already made famous, with his cover of it on the 1991 album *Warm Your Heart*. A week after Neville's appearance on NBC, Newman performed his own song, as part of *Shelter from the Storm: A Concert for the Gulf Coast*, broadcast to over 100 countries. The 30-year-old composition was now indelibly associated with Katrina and its relief efforts.

But, as the title suggests, Newman's song told of an event that happened 80 years earlier. The great flood of 1927 changed the American south forever. After a heavy spring rain, the Mississippi burst its banks, covering land from Illinois down to Memphis with several feet of water. Louisiana was next. A clique of bankers and governors blew a levee above New Orleans to spare the city. The swollen river was diverted across the farms and plantations of Plaquemines Parish, and even as far west as the parish of Evangeline, leaving many homeless and without compensation. As the waters rose, hundreds lost their lives and millions their livelihoods. "The cotton fields were wiped out... disemploying hundreds of thousands of black field-workers," said Newman. "They all moved north and were greeted with open arms right across America."

After the waters subsided, many wrote and sang of the tragedy. One piece of musical reportage written that year, Kansas Joe and Memphis Minnie's 'When the Levee Breaks', was later made famous by Led Zeppelin. The great delta bluesman, Big Bill Broonzy, recalled that one record company executive promised $500 for the best song about the flood. The singer Bessie Smith won, with her 'Back Water Blues'. "It had more feelings to it, and it had more sense too," said Broonzy. "I don't think nobody in the world ever sang it like Bessie."

'Louisiana 1927', delivered in the voice of one who escaped the rising waters, is mesmerising. The opening plangent chords recall America's great parlour songwriter of the nineteenth century, Stephen Foster. "The intro to it, that sort of plantation music felt right to me," said Newman. It swells into an unbearable refrain. Newman first recorded it at Amigo Studios, Hollywood early in 1973. As a single, issued in 1975, it did nothing, but it remains a pivotal track on his album of "Southern discomfort", *Good Old Boys*, and one of his greatest songs.

YOU'VE GOT THE LOVE
FLORENCE + THE MACHINE (2008)
Original by Candi Staton (1986)

Three times a hit in the Nineties and endlessly remixed before landing in the lap of Florence + the Machine, 'You've Got the Love' dates back to 1986, when it was titled 'You Got the Love'. The southern soul star Candi Staton first recorded it, as the theme for a video about the world's fattest man and his endeavour to lose weight. In return for her vocal services the programme makers donated half the publishing rights to Staton. It was issued as a seven-inch in 1986, credited to the anonymous label act the Source (featuring Candi Staton), with composition by Anthony B. Stephens, Arnecia Michelle Harris and John Bellamy. When a soul/gospel mix of the song reached the UK Top Five in 1991, Staton was contacted. She initially denied all knowledge of the song. "Then I got off the phone and realised – it was the one from the diet video! Which was never supposed to be put on a record at all," she said.

Staton eventually received healthy royalties from her recording, which were accelerated when Florence + the Machine returned it to the charts in 2009. Florence Welch had remembered it from raves in the early Nineties. "We were thinking of an amazing cover we could do, and I thought of Candi Staton," she said. The band premiered their version at Bestival 2008. "I was dressed as a genie sea-monster," Welch said. "I remember looking at my guitarist as we played the first chords, and then there was the reaction and it was like tearing ourselves open and just exploding on the crowd."

The studio version was recorded with Charlie Hugall producing and features harpist Tom Monger. It was first issued as the B-side of the single 'Dog Days Are Over' in 2008, until popularity ensured its reissue as a digital download the following year. It finally charted towards the end of 2009, boosted by its inclusion as a bonus track on the band's debut album *Lungs*. Welch took the opportunity to correct the grammar in the title. Joss Stone, who didn't, included a brassy version on her album *Colour Me Free!* Kasabian have also tackled it and in 2009 Florence + the Machine's version was beautifully reconfigured by fellow south Londoners The xx, who turn the song into an ambient, mumbling mash-up.

YOU'VE GOT A FRIEND
JAMES TAYLOR (1971)
Original by Carole King (1971)

During the early Seventies, there was a feeling amongst the countercultural generation that "friends were the new family". In response to this, Carole King had written a hymn to companionship, but was unsure if it rang true. Despite her pedigree as a key composer of postwar American popular song, King was not a natural lyricist. Around Christmas 1970, she sat at her Steinway grand and played the new song to her producer, Lou Adler. "I have feelings of wondering about whether it's going to make it or not," King said, recalling how she felt at the play-through. "All the big insecurities really happen when I'm writing the song." Was it any good? King remembered Adler's unequivocal, one-word response on hearing the song for the first time: "Yeah!"

Still unconvinced, she also tried it out on her co-lyricist, Toni Stern, who thought it was "too obvious". Another songwriter, Cynthia Weil, first heard King play it in her apartment and considered it "too long". The song swayed from minor to major, and back to minor. It hit all the right keys, but was 'You've Got a Friend' really any good? The answer came when a young musician, James Taylor, heard it. "Damn! Why didn't *I* write that?" declared Taylor, then beginning to flex his own songwriting muscle. In January 1971, Taylor's unfussy acoustic guitar backed King on her version of the song, for what would become a defining album of the era, *Tapestry*.

King and Taylor, with the help of the musician Danny Kortchmar, vocalist Merry Clayton and a string quartet, nailed the song in one take. But the song was just *too* good, as far as Taylor was concerned. It needed to be done again. The same month, he appropriated the song for himself, making it a US Number One and earning Grammys for both singer and writer.

Taylor was almost pipped to the post. Before he could get his version out, it was also recorded by Dusty Springfield, just as she was running into problems with her label. Her doe-eyed, soulful cover lay unissued in the Atlantic Records vaults until 1999, when it appeared as a bonus track on the reissue of *Dusty in Memphis*. It's since been recorded by everyone from Al Green to McFly and King's original is now accompanied on reissues of *Tapestry* by an early live version of the song.

LET'S STICK TOGETHER
BRYAN FERRY (1976)
Original by Wilbert Harrison (1962)

Bryan Ferry's biggest solo success was a faithful take on a half-forgotten classic. In the early Sixties, the R&B singer Wilbert Harrison was struggling to find a decent follow up to his 1959 Number One, a slow-beat take on an early Leiber and Stoller number, 'Kansas City', a song soon to feature in the Beatles' repertoire. Eventually, in 1962, Harrison released 'Let's Stick Together' on the tiny New York label Fury. It was a self-penned tribute to marital fidelity. Ventilated by a blast of raw harmonica, 'Let's Stick Together' was a sharp dancefloor filler but failed to chart.

Harrison was undeterred and at the other end of the decade he resurrected his flop, slowing it down and retitling it as a consciousness-raising blues shuffle, 'Let's Work Together', thus providing an international hit for Canned Heat in 1970. The blueprint for the rewrite was overlooked in the makeover, although not by Roxy Music's suave frontman. Ferry preferred Harrison's rough and ready original and in the spring of 1976, with Roxy Music on ice and punk skulking in the shadows, he cut his own version of 'Let's Stick Together'. A roster of guest musicians were booked: the guitarists Chris Spedding and (an uncredited) David O'List; Roxy's drummer, Paul Thompson, and King Crimson old boys John Wetton and Mel Collins. The sessions were produced by the Sex Pistol's soon-to-be producer of choice, Chris Thomas.

As 'Let's Stick Together' climbed the charts that summer, Roxy Music confirmed persistent rumours that they would be going their separate ways. The single has become as famous for the video as for the music itself. Shot in the Rainbow Room, on the top floor of the London fashion store Biba, it featured Ferry's then girlfriend, the model Jerry Hall, whose Texan yelps gave the record its gimmicky hook. It was given added sheen in a 1988 remix, when it revisited the charts, and Bob Dylan issued his own version, on the album *Down in the Groove*. Harrison continued to perform his song well into the Eighties and died aged 65 in 1994.

SUMMERTIME BLUES
THE WHO (1970)
Original by Eddie Cochran (1958)

Eddie Cochran, the first rock star to die on British soil, inspired a generation of young guitarists. George Harrison followed his tour around the UK, and Marc Bolan even claimed he once carried Cochran's orange Gretsch to a waiting car outside the Hackney Empire. In April 1960 the Ford Consul taking Cochran to Heathrow spun off the road and tangled with a concrete post near Chippenham, Wiltshire, killing the 21-year-old and wounding his fellow passengers, Sharon Sheeley and Gene Vincent.

Penned by the Eddie and his manager, Jerry Capehart, and apparently taking less than an hour to compose, 'Summertime Blues' was recorded at Hollywood's Gold Star studios and is perhaps Cochran's best-known song. Capehart reckoned they wrote it because no-one else had come up with a song about the hardships of summer. In truth it is more than that – it's a rebel yell against the establishment, parents and working for "the Man"; the original teenage anthem. Originally intended as a B-side, 'Summertime Blues' turned out to be Cochran's breakthrough, making the charts in 1958.

Forever a key influence on a generation of rockers and covered by T. Rex and Blue Cheer, amongst others, it's the Who's version of this musical sunblock which really kicks the summertime blues into touch. The Who loved Cochran and introduced 'Summertime Blues' into their own live set early in their career. The best version can be found on their concert album *Live at Leeds*, issued in 1970, where Pete Townshend riffs around Cochran's original and the vocals are handled by Roger Daltry and bassist John Entwistle. Issued as a single, it was, naturally, a hit in the summer of that year.

There are many other well-known covers of Cochran songs.

Rod Stewart's 'Cut Across Shorty' was a high point of his 1970 album *Gasoline Alley*. Cochran's posthumous release 'Three Steps to Heaven' was revived in 1975 by the clumsily-named Showaddywaddy, who bounded on to the stage like a gang of primary-coloured teds. And after John Lydon quit, the Sex Pistols resorted to Cochran covers, making hits of 'C'mon Everybody' and 'Somethin' Else' in 1978.

Perhaps most significantly though, it was Cochran's 'Twenty Flight Rock' with which a young Paul McCartney wowed John Lennon, that summer's day in 1957 when they met for the first time. Lennon was so impressed that Macca knew all the chords *and* the words, he invited him into the band. It was later recorded by McCartney on his "Russian album" *CHOBA B CCCP*.

A GOOD YEAR FOR THE ROSES
ELVIS COSTELLO (1981)
Original by George Jones (1970)

Elvis Costello's digression into country and western for the great covers album *Almost Blue* produced one of his biggest hits, making the Top 10 in October 1981. 'A Good Year for the Roses' was written by the songwriter Jerry Chesnut. "I was having trouble with my roses," recalls Chesnut, casting his mind back to the late Sixties. "One of them was an Oklahoma rose. They'd get these great big buds on them which would just fall off. I called the garden centre and asked them what was wrong. They said, 'nothing – we've had a lot of rain. It's just not a good year for the roses.'" In 1970 Chesnut was in his writing room and he remembered the comment. "It crossed my mind, what if it was a great year for roses and everything else had gone to pot?"

It was a song waiting to be written. "The roses are blooming like crazy. A man loves his wife but she's leaving, and the baby is crying," explains Chesnut. The twist is, the woman is walking out on her child: a sideways take on a familiar theme. Chesnut demoed it that night. Across town, the singer George Jones was at the Ramada Inn. "George called me and said, man I need a hit," says Chesnut. 'Roses' was exactly what Jones wanted. He recorded it at Nashville's Columbia studios, with the producer Bob Moore, and the record topped the US country charts in 1971. Ten years later, Costello rolled up at the very same studio to record *Almost Blue*, his collection of country crossovers, with the producer Billy Sherrill.

Chesnut was present at the session, as he had been when Jones cut the original. He loved Costello's rendition of his song. Costello was as surprised as anyone when it was a hit: "If me just recording 'Good Year For The Roses', whether or not it was a good record or not, had anybody buy a George Jones record, then my work here is done," he said. It's also been covered by Counting Crows and Richard Thompson, and Jones re-recorded it in 1994 as a duet with new-country singer Alan Jackson. Chesnut has since reworked it for female singers: "I changed just a line or two and made a girl's song out of it. It wound up being twice as strong, I believe"

ONLY LOVE CAN BREAK YOUR HEART
SAINT ETIENNE (1990)
Original by Neil Young (1970)

On the face of it, a dance version of a Neil Young song was never going to work. And there are plenty who say it doesn't. Neither Young's confessional, singer-songwriter drone nor his tendency towards gingham-edged grunge seemed compatible with Saint Etienne's interest in house, techno and indie pop. 'Only Love Can Break Your Heart' had already been covered, as a soft-funk smooch by Elkie Brooks, in the late Seventies. For the Saint Etienne cover, Bob Stanley and Pete Wiggs updated the love lorn ballad once more, ditching Young's ragged, southern waltz in favour of a smoking, four-beats-to-the-bar, piano-driven disco groove. Vocals were supplied by Moira Lambert of the indie band Faith Over Reason.

The second single on the fledgling Heavenly Records, 'Only Love Can Break Your Heart' was all over dancefloors in the summer of 1990. It was recorded by Stanley and Wiggs for just £200. They chose a cover as their first single, they claimed, partly because the art-punks Psychic TV had covered the same song, but mainly because they hadn't written any original material for the session before they booked it. "We were thinking of doing 'Ambulance Blues' by Neil Young, but it was too long. And it was too difficult," claimed Stanley. Reissued in 1991 to trail the band's first album, *Foxbase Alpha*, it was a surprise debut chart hit for the London band, becoming only the second Young cover to make the Top 40, after Prelude's 1974 a cappella take on 'After the Goldrush'.

'Only Love Can Break Your Heart' began life as a track on Young's largely acoustic album *After the Gold Rush* – the one that also features the iconic 'Southern Man' – and was issued as a single in the autumn of 1970, charting only in the US.

There was speculation when the song first appeared that the subject was Young's bandmate, Stephen Stills, then embarking on an affair with the singer Rita Coolidge. Although Stills would record a cover of the song himself in the Eighties, Young confirmed on stage during a 1977 concert that in fact he had penned it for another friend, the singer Graham Nash, then in the throes of a painful and much publicised split with Joni Mitchell. The song has been often performed by Young over the years, especially during his tenure as one quarter of Crosby, Stills, Nash and Young.

ROCKIN' ALL OVER THE WORLD
STATUS QUO (1977)
Original by John Fogerty (1975)

Status Quo's signature song is not quite the thumbs-in-denim-pockets head-shaker their version might suggest. It was written by John Fogerty, the frontman with Creedence Clearwater Revival. After Creedence's demise in 1972, leaving in their wake the driving 'Proud Mary' and 'Bad Moon Rising', Fogerty launched a solo career with an album of covers, which flopped. He followed it with a self-titled set of original material. Sales of the second album were also slender, but *John Fogerty* (also known as "Shep", after the cute collie dog pictured on the cover), contained a sleeping giant. In September 1975, 'Rockin' All Over the World', rolling country-blues with a serrated twang, was issued as a single, and radio stations loved it.

Cut to Status Quo's guitarist Rick Parfitt, cruising through the night. "It was 4 o'clock in the morning. I was driving my Porsche and this song came on the radio… I just loved this song," he recalled. 'Rockin' All Over the World' had all the hallmarks of a Quo classic: notably a relentless three-chord rumble and a good tune. It was catchy from the start and Parfitt and fellow Quo frontman, Francis Rossi, made it the slick title track to Quo's 1977 album. It's still their most successful live number and in 1985 was chosen as the natural opener for the Live Aid concert, becoming the event's anthem. "God, I wish we could have written this song!" commented Rossi. In 1988 they tried, reworking it as 'Running All Over the World', for Sport Aid '88, the lyrics appropriately altered.

After 'Rockin' All Over the World', it took Fogerty nine years to get back on track with a third solo album. Legal problems delayed a follow-up when his band's former management filed a lawsuit against the singer, claiming that his new material sounded too similar to his songwriting for Creedence. In the meantime, Quo made his song their own. Fogerty could hardly complain and gave them full credit when he played it live: "This was a big hit for Status Quo in England, but you never heard it here," he told an American audience oblivious to Quo's UK chart successes. The song has attracted others, including the Beach Boy's Carl Wilson and Bruce Springsteen, who featured it as a rowdy tour staple during the mid-Eighties.

STEP ON
HAPPY MONDAYS (1990)
Original by John Kongos (1971)

The Johannesburg-born John Kongos cut a string of psychedelic flops for the Pye subsidiary Piccadilly in the mid Sixties, before signing to the independent Fly. 'He's Gonna Step On You Again' was his first release on the new label in 1971 – a Lennonesque protest anthem, warning against white man's appropriation of native territory.

The pioneering sound was largely the work of producer Gus Dudgeon. "The whole record is built on a loop, lifted from an African tribal dance recorded in some jungle somewhere," he told *Sound on Sound* magazine. Dudgeon ran the two-and-a-half-bar loop through the mixing desk and instructed his studio musicians to play over it. "The drummer was, like, 'what? It's got drums on it already!' All the time they were doing it I was terrified. No one had ever done it before, I was thinking I was going to have my arse sued off, but the point was you could never have faked it." Dudgeon dubbed on the rest of the musicians and Kongos's vocals. *"The Guiness Book of Records* have actually sent me a fax saying that they recognise it as the first sample ever used on record."

Dudgeon went on to produce hit albums for Elton John, while Kongos gave up performing to become a successful engineer and jingle writer. Their percussive collaboration inspired early Adam Ant and Bow Wow Wow and, in the late Eighties, a slack happy Shaun Ryder. On the Happy Mondays' version, topped and tailed as 'Step On', Ryder moans "You're twisting my melon, man" and turns a clarion call for land rights into a northern English dance classic. Boasting more baggy funk than jungle rumbling, it lollopped into the Top Five in 1990. In a further homage to the curly-haired Kongos, the Happy Mondays also covered his follow-up single, probably the only chart hit about South African witchcraft, the splendid 'Tokoloshe Man'.

Robert Webb

THE DAYS OF PEARLY SPENCER
MARC ALMOND (1989)
Original by David McWilliams (1967)

The death of singer-songwriter David McWilliams in 2002 at the age of 56 went largely unnoticed, at least outside of his native Belfast. A childhood neighbour of George Best, and a talented footballer himself, McWilliams was a private and self-effacing musician. He is chiefly remembered for one song – 1967's haunting 'The Days of Pearly Spencer'. It was one of the more sober releases of the Summer of Love, a tale of tenements, dirty streets and an urban down-and-out heading for the cemetery gates. A swirl of strings whistle around the tenement blocks – not even a daisy can make it through the broken concrete. This is the flipside of the Swinging Sixties.

McWilliams wrote the song after befriending a homeless man in Ballymena, as a reflection of his "deep humanity and empathy with those who live on the margins of society". Missing the charts by a whisker, it was a turntable hit and got a lot of airplay. It was a longtime favourite with former Soft Cell singer Marc Almond, who first heard it on Radio Caroline as an adolescent. He recorded his version in 1991 for the album *Tenement Symphony*, which included his arrangement of another 1967 hit, Scott Walker's 'Jacky'.

Both covers entered the charts, and helped to establish Almond as a solo artist. His production of 'Pearly Spencer' is arguably the better, sensibly junking McWilliams' dated megaphone-effect vocals in the chorus. Almond certainly enjoyed reviving the song. "Was I tempted to sing 'Pearly Necklace' in its place? I think a few people have probably done that themselves," he said. The track not only provided the title for Almond's album but, to alleviate the pessimism of the original, Almond added his own verse to update the story, in which the protagonist looks back to the desperate days when shoeless feet were wedged in death's door. In Almond's version, Pearly Spencer got lucky.

HANDBAGS AND GLADRAGS
THE STEREOPHONICS (2001)
Original by Double Feature/Chris Farlowe (1967)

The short-lived but trend-setting Immediate Records, launched by Rolling Stones' manager Andrew Loog Oldham in the mid Sixties, has been a surprisingly rich wellspring for cover artists. Soul/pop diva P.P. Arnold's 'Angel of the Morning', released on the label in 1968, was reconfigured by Shaggy as 'Angel'. In 2001, the Stereophonics topped the tree with 'Handbags and Gladrags', first aired by Immediate mainstay Chris Farlowe in 1967. This song was penned by Manfred Mann vocalist Mike D'Abo and originally recorded for Deram by a sunk-without-trace Birmingham act, Double Feature. But before the duo's version could make it from the pressing plant, the wily Oldham had Farlowe's version in the shops. While Farlowe hit Number One, Double Feature's single was melted down (although a few copies inevitably survived: one can even be seen spinning on YouTube).

It's an early cover of 'Handbags' by Rod Stewart, however, that inspired Welsh popsters Stereophonics. D'Abo is clearly delighted with its resurrection. In a letter of praise to the trio's frontman, Kelly Jones, posted on the Manfreds' website, he tells the story behind his masterpiece: "[Rod Stewart] wanted to record the song as well," he explains, "Unfortunately, since I had promised it to Chris, Rod had to settle for another of my songs, 'Little Miss Understood'. Rod made me promise to let him record H&G once he got himself an album deal." Stewart got his chance a couple of years later and included it on his debut album *An Old Raincoat Never Lets You Down*. He also called on D'Abo for the memorable piano and wind arrangement, lacking in Farlowe's original. "This session came together at very short notice, with what subsequently became the Faces as the rhythm section," recalls D'Abo. Although now better known than the Farlowe original, Stewart's definitive punt at 'Handbags' was never a hit.

The Stereophonics are, unsurprisingly, huge fans of early Rod and the Faces and cut their note-perfect doppelganger of the Stewart copy after establishing it as a live favourite and performing it live on *Later with Jools Holland*. The song was also used as the theme to the BBC's top-drawer comedy *The Office*.

NO MORE "I LOVE YOUS"
ANNIE LENNOX (1995)
Original by the Lover Speaks (1986)

On her second solo outing, *Medusa*, Annie Lennox tackles a few of her favourite compositions by other people. The making of the album, a dinner-party favourite in the mid Nineties, was "truly a labour of love", as Lennox puts it in her liner notes. "A selection of songs I have been drawn to for all kinds of reasons." Among the hit-and-miss covers is the fragile heartbreaker, "No More 'I Love Yous'". It was the least-known of *Medusa's* lovingly-chosen tracks at the time of the album's release and was first recorded a decade earlier by the curiously-named duo, the Lover Speaks, aka David Freeman and Joseph Hughes.

Freeman and Hughes were at a loose end after their punk band the Flys finally hit the windshield. They took on the name the Lover Speaks, from a line in a Roland Barthes discourse. Hughes sent a demo tape of their efforts to the Eurythmics' Dave Stewart, who nodded his approval and forwarded it to Chrissie Hynde of the Pretenders. Hynde, in turn, spooled the cassette on to her producer, Jimmy Iovine, whose client roster also included Patti Smith and Tom Petty. A deal was struck with A&M and Iovine took the duo out to Los Angeles to record. Released in 1986, the Lover Speaks' self-titled album contained one great, swooping ballad: a poetic croon about demons in the bedroom.

Freeman's guitar chimes around the drummer's hollow smack and the whole arrangement hangs on an infectious "Doo-bi-doo-bi-doo-doo-doo-oh" backing line. When Stewart designated the song one of his tips for the top on an MTV show, people took note. Under Stewart's patronage, Freeman and Hughes hit the road, opening for the Eurythmics on their 1986 tour. But their single struggled to peak at Number 58 in the charts and was quickly forgotten.

A&M lost interest and the lover spoke no more. Until 1995,

that is, when Lennox was casting around for songs for *Medusa* and resurrected 'No More "I Love Yous"'. As the album's lead single, it settled just shy of the Number One spot, turning it into something of a solo signature tune. So closely is the song now identified with Lennox, that few other people have attempted it.

SAY YOU DON'T MIND
COLIN BLUNSTONE (1971)
Original by the Denny Laine (1967)

When the Zombies split, sensing that their time of the season had finally come and gone (leaving behind the posthumous, wondrous *Odessey and Oracle*), their lead singer, Colin Blunstone, threw in the towel and took a clerical job in an insurance firm, handling burglary claims. Blunstone was coaxed back into the studio in 1971 to record a solo album, *One Year*, with the help of other former Zombies, now trading under the name of Argent. 'Say You Don't Mind' was one of those songs he had kicked around in the Zombies, but never got around to recording properly. A quirky, melodic sliver of mid-Sixties pop from the pen of Denny Laine, it was the perfect coda to *One Year* and, issued as a single, charmed its way up the charts in the winter of 1972.

Its success was long overdue. Back in the spring of 1967, as the Beatles were polishing off *Sgt Pepper*, Laine was busy assembling the Electric String Band, his first group after quitting as lead singer of the Moody Blues. Before the band took off, Laine cut 'Say You Don't Mind', for the Deram label. It's one of the great neglected pop singles of the day. "'Say You Don't Mind' had a very good underground following," Laine recalled. "I did it with strings and it had that string band feel, which is why I put that band together, to sort of cover that style." Laine had commissioned a prominent London session player to score the strings – the soon to be Led Zeppelin bassist, John Paul Jones. But not even Jones's magic touch could make the song a hit.

When Blunstone took it to the top five years later, in an intimate arrangement by Chris Gunning, its composer was naturally delighted. "That kind of generated a little bit of a market for me," said Laine, by now part of Wings. Blunstone claims his arranger was only paid £15 for his work on the song – but that

171

he was even worse off. "When Denny admitted that through some strange publishing agreement he didn't receive one penny for writing the song," said Blunstone, "I felt quite relieved that I could counter his claim by saying truthfully I also didn't receive a penny in royalties for the track."

RED RED WINE
UB40 (1983)
Original by Neil Diamond (1968)

Negus Diamond was the reggae songwriter responsible for the Sixties dancehall classic 'Red Red Wine' – at least, that's what UB40 initially assumed as they were gathering songs for their 1983 covers album, *Labour of Love*. "We only knew it as a reggae song," said the band's lead singer, Ali Campbell. Their rapper, Astro, concurred: "Even when we saw the writing credit, which said 'N. Diamond', we thought it was a Jamaican artist." "Negus" Diamond seemed likely, they concluded. The version they were familiar with, courtesy of reggae artist Tony Tribe, was in fact, as they later discovered, a cover of a country-flavoured flop by the middle-of-the-road balladeer Neil Diamond.

The original was cut in 1968, as Diamond was a struggling singer-songwriter, but stalled in lower regions of the Billboard charts. The song wasn't completely overlooked, however. In London the same year, Jimmy James and the Vagabonds grazed the UK Top 40 with a leisurely ska version. In 1969, with Jamaican rhythms on the rise, Trojan Records were handing out reggae arrangements of contemporary American releases. Tribe, born Tony Mossop in Kingston Jamaica, but now living in London, had abandoned his job in the post room of the Jamaican High Commission to sing gospel and reggae full time. With the producer Dandy Livingstone at the controls and a roster of studio session men, including Rod Stewart's bassist, Philip Chen, Tribe jettisoned Diamond's melancholic baritone for his perky, definitive reading of 'Red Red Wine'.

Tribe sadly died in a road accident in 1970, after making 'Red Red Wine' Trojan's first – and his only – chart entry (on the Down Town subsidiary). His single was a huge club hit as well, making a particular impact on a young Ali Campbell, who sought out anything Trojan related. Fourteen years later, UB40 were working on *Labour of Love*. Mixed with the help of the Jamaican producer Mikey Dread, their rendition of 'Red Red Wine', a facsimile of Tribe's take on the song (complete with copycat steel drums), was earmarked as a single and swept to Number One in September 1983. Diamond was so impressed at the way his half-forgotten composition had been resurrected he took to performing a live arrangement in the mould of the Birmingham beatsters – occasionally even attempting an ill-advised Astro-style rap mid-song.

ACROSS THE UNIVERSE
DAVID BOWIE (1975)
Original by the Beatles (1967)

As David Bowie was recording his soul album *Young Americans*, with John Lennon helping out on backing vocals and guitar, it seemed natural to try a Beatles number. They settled on 'Across the Universe'. "It's one of my favourite songs," said Bowie. Although Bowie wasn't too happy with the result, the former Beatle loved it. "I'd never done a good version of that song myself," Lennon later said.

Written by Lennon and recorded by the Beatles in February 1968, 'Across the Universe' was the original pop fund-raiser. Lennon once pitched the song, which some heard as meandering and platitudinous, as the next Beatles' single, but lost out to an unsympathetic Paul McCartney and the pummelling 'Lady Madonna'. Instead it was donated to the World Wildlife Fund (WWF), at Spike Milligan's behest, for the 1969 charity album *No One's Gonna Change Our World*. The spiritual strumalong nestled awkwardly amid comedy rousers by Bruce Forsythe and Rolf Harris.

The lyrics came to Lennon as he lay awake one night in 1967, after arguing with Cynthia Lennon. "It drove me out of bed," he said, recalling how he threw back the sheets to commit a rough draft to paper. "I didn't want to write it. I was just slightly irritable and couldn't get to sleep." The song found its proper shape following Lennon's sojourn with the Maharishi Mahesh Yogi and was finally given official Beatles release two years later with *Let It Be*, where it sat just as uncomfortably as it had on the WWF compilation. In the hands of the producer Phil Spector, Lennon's woozy, wordy lullaby was stretched and smothered in strings. Many hated it, McCartney included, although it resurfaced on the Beatles' "Blue Album", *1967–70* in 1973. An early take closed *Anthology 2* in 1996 and the original mix was exhumed for the 2003 revisionist project *Let It Be... Naked*.

It's been covered by many, including Rufus Wainwright and Laibach, and also helped inspire Pink Floyd's 1971 track 'Echoes' – whose lyrics can happily be sung to the melody of 'Across the Universe'. Roger Waters even tweaked Lennon's line "exciting and inviting me" into "inviting and inciting me".

(I CAN'T GET NO) SATISFACTION
DEVO (1977)
Original by the Rolling Stones (1965)

Along with an earlier reconfiguration of the song by the Residents, issued in 1976, Devo's cover of 'Satisfaction' is one of the most extraordinary versions of any Rolling Stones track. Mick Jagger was all for it, apparently: it was, according to his lawyer, likely to give him considerable financial satisfaction if it were a hit. And it surely would be a hit, wouldn't it?

In 1977 Devo were the art-punk satirists most likely to. They came out of Akron, Ohio dressed in flowerpot hats and tangerine boiler suits, with the slogan "Are we not men? We are Devo!" like the dysfunctional Midwest cousins of David Byrne. When they got their nimble fingers on '(I Can't Get No) Satisfaction' they retitled it '(I Can't Get Me No) Satisfaction' and duly transformed it from one of cocksure frustration into a deadpan, mechanical jerk. Devo stripped the song back to its bare bones – and then rearranged the skeleton to create a wholly new animal.

Noticed by Eno and David Bowie and consequently signed to Stiff records in the UK, Devo and their decidedly strange single was a small hit, just nudging the Top 40. It was a Number One in Yugoslavia, though, but perhaps overall not the smash Jagger and his accountant were anticipating.

The song itself was written by Jagger and Keith Richards and was, as Richards puts it, "the track that launched us into global fame". Famously, Richards claimed he wrote the tune in his sleep. Waking in the night in his St John's Wood apartment, the bleary-eyed guitarist committed the melody to his cassette recorder with an acoustic and turned over to resume his slumbers. The following morning he had forgotten the nocturnal interruption but noticed that the new tape he had put into the machine the night before had spooled through.

"Then I pushed rewind and there was 'Satisfaction'," he says.

Jagger penned the lyrics in Florida, lounging by a pool, and four days later the Stones were at Chess studio in Chicago, cutting an acoustic demo. The song's trademark fuzz tone was created across the country at RCA in Hollywood. It sounded, in its day, like nothing had before – the only point of reference was Dave Davies's frayed chops on early Kinks records. But where the distorted fuzzed-up guitar came in the song, Richards had initially envisaged a horn riff. The precise sound he wanted would have to wait for Otis Redding's brassy cover version later that year.

MONEY (THAT'S WHAT I WANT)
THE FLYING LIZARDS (1979)
Original by Barrett Strong (1959)

The original of 'Money (That's What I Want)', by former gospel singer Barrett Strong, was technically the first hit for Motown's Berry Gordy. Initially it been released on Gordy's Anna label in 1959, just as Tamla was getting underway. Gordy wrote the song with Janie Bradford – a Tamla, later Motown, songwriter – and Strong took it to the charts, spawning hundreds of versions. Before the Flying Lizards came along it had – not unlike real money – passed through very many hands, from Freddie and the Dreamers to John Lee Hooker. But without the cover by the Beatles in 1963, on their second album, it may well have fallen by the wayside.

The Flying Lizards was a late-Seventies loose collective of experimental artists and musicians, centred around producer David Cunningham – a man who was equal parts Phil Spector, Donna Summer and Marcel Duchamp. Cunningham employed several female singers for the Flying Lizards: the precise, flat vocals on 'Money' were those of Deborah Evans-Strickland.

The pianist on the recording, Julian Marshall, remembers Cunningham playing him the original to refresh his memory. Then one microphone was placed in the piano and another on the floor, by a metronome. In order to get a decent percussion sound they threw in objects to dampen the piano strings – sheet music, a glass ashtray, rubber toys, a cassette recorder, a telephone directory. Cunningham hit a borrowed snare drum and a tambourine, overdubbing them in a echo-filled room next to the studio lavatory. Evans-Strickland recorded her vocals in "a freezing cold meat fridge" in Brixton, south London, as she recalls.

After two takes it was declared a wrap. "I was slightly amazed: it sounded fairly wrong," said Marshall. "But the next time I heard it, at Utopia, where [Cunningham] was cutting it, it sounded fantastic." And how much did they spend? "It was very low budget and only cost £6.50 to make," reckoned Evans-Strickland. It was punk's DIY ethos down to a tee.

The low-tech, clattery cover version was a surprise hit in the summer of 1979 and their one and only hit continues to appear on movie soundtracks. The band liked covers. Their third, and final, album, issued in 1984, consisted entirely of their own idiosyncratic take on songs such as James Brown's 'Sex Machine', and Leonard Cohen's 'Suzanne'.

WITHOUT YOU
HARRY NILSSON (1971)
Original by Badfinger (1970)

It must be the saddest song of all. 'Without You' is not just the paradigmatic breakup song, but it seemed that, for a while at least, death stalked it, prompting some to conclude that the song is perhaps cursed. It started life as harmony-driven guitar pop by the Welsh group Badfinger, the first band signed to the Beatles' Apple label. Written by frontmen Pete Ham and Tom Evans, in cramped digs in Golders Green, north London, it was based on real events in their respective personal lives. It was effectively a medley of two separate songs. Ham's 'If it's Love' was originally penned for his girlfriend, Beverley Tucker, but was essentially no more than a bunch of verses. The necessary chorus was supplied by Evans who's own song had the line "I can't live if living is without you", which he dedicated to his wife. Evans and Ham welded together their two compositions to create the heartbreaking 'Without You', with its crescendo chorus. It was good – although Ham dismissed it at the time as "corny". Recorded in 1970 for the Badfinger album *No Dice*, the track didn't even make seven-inch in its day.

Indeed it may have remained stuck in a byway of British power-pop had it not been for Harry Nilsson. Championed by the Beatles in the late Sixties (he even recorded a three-minute medley of 22 Beatles songs centred on 'You Can't Do That'), Nilsson had heard 'Without You' at a party and thought it was John Lennon. He eventually tracked it down and took it to his producer, Richard Perry, recording his version for the album *Nilsson Schmilsson*. He injected a little more melodrama into his cover, yet managed to retain the playful, love-letter feel of the original. When Evans first heard it, he reported that the band were "freaked out".

It swiftly topped charts around the world and unavoidably

became Nilsson's signature tune. Covered by many down the years, it finally fell to Mariah Carey to revive the song in the Nineties, with a version that seems to be universally despised – at least by those who know and love the earlier recordings. Carey packs her rendition with unnecessary vocal gymnastics, apparently failing to notice that, with 'Without You', less is more.

Her cover version came as Nilsson's early death from a heart attack was announced. But it is the double suicides of the song's writers which make the lyrics of the song so appallingly prophetic. After Nilsson's was a global hit, the band hit the buffers in a tangle of mismanagement and embezzled royalties, which dragged the band through the courts. As a result Ham slid into terminal depression, hanging himself in April 1975. Evans, who suffered from mood swings and could never shake off the death of his bandmate, took his own life eight years later.

HALLELUJAH
JEFF BUCKLEY (1994)
Original by Leonard Cohen (1984)

The extraordinary success of 'Hallelujah' is down to a combination of high(ish) art and lowbrow culture. Written by Leonard Cohen, and buried on his 1984 album *Various Positions*, it was revived by John Cale, who took to performing it live with just a piano for accompaniment: it concluded his 1992 album *Fragments of a Rainy Season*. Jeff Buckley, the son of singer-songwriter Tim Buckley, heard Cale's version and loved it, recording his own cover with an electric guitar in place of Cale's piano, for the album *Grace* – which turned out to be Buckley's only release during his short life.

Although not put out as a single during Buckley's lifetime, it ultimately became his best-known recording, punting the hitherto little-heard song onto various "Best Songs of All Time" lists (*Rolling Stone* magazine placed it at number 259). Buckley's suitably reverential rendition gets to the heart of the song: on its release in 1994 it marked him as a singer of prodigious talent.

But before work on a follow up could be completed, Buckley drowned in the Mississippi, in 1997, after swimming with his boots on, apparently entering the water singing Led Zeppelin's 'Whole Lotta Love'. Eleven years later, his version of 'Hallelujah' found its way up to the Number One spot on the iTunes chart, having sold 178,000 downloads for the week. What propelled it there was an unlikely pair of performances on two reality TV shows. In the UK, *X Factor* winner Alexandra Burke (or the show's producers) selected it for her gospel-tinged finale and she subsequently claimed the 2008 UK Christmas Number One with it. Jason Castro performed a similar feat in the US, after aping Buckely for *American Idol*, although never quite making the top notes.

Both covers prompted Buckley fans, not unreasonably, to launch a campaign for his version to join them at the top of the charts. Gaining support through social media, the Buckley single, reissued as a download only, was on the Number Two spot in the Christmas week. Extraordinarily, the original by Cohen also crept into the charts, settling at Number 38 in the UK, thus providing the song's composer with his only British chart hit to date.

HOW CAN YOU MEND A BROKEN HEART
AL GREEN (1972)
Original by the Bee Gees (1971)

First offered to cardiganed crooner Andy Williams – but presumably rejected by him – the Gibb brothers wound up recording what turned out to be one of their finest compositions themselves. It was written in 1970, by Barry and Robin Gibb, with some help from their brother Maurice, probably at Barry's Holland Park home. Writing took about half an hour, according to Robin. Once Williams had declined it, it was slated as the opener to the Bee Gees' loose concept album *Trafalgar* the following year. Although it failed to trouble the UK charts at all, the single became the trio's first US Number One.

Where most heard a syrupy, quivering ballad, Al Green sensed soul. His cover, for the album *Let's Stay Together*, was a career highpoint for the Memphis singer and is, quite possibly, one of the greatest things he has done. Green recorded his version at Royal Recording Studios in Memphis, with producer Willie Mitchell at the helm, for release on the Hi Records label.

As with so many Bee Gees songs and other artists, Green shapes it to his own style and moulds a torch ballad which surpasses the original in every way possible. Charles Hodges' Hammond organ is crucial, providing the background wash to Green's delicate brushwork. The other two Hodges brothers, Leroy and Teenie – along with Charles aka the Hi Rhythm Section – sit in on bass and guitar respectively, neatly echoing the three-brothers line-up of the original version.

It's since been covered by many, including Diana Krall, Cher, Michael Bublé and even the "fourth Bee Gee", the late Andy Gibb. Green still enjoys performing 'How Can You Mend a

Broken Heart'. The only thing that puts him off, he says, is the way his audience always tries to sing along – badly. "They sound like some little chickens down there," he once commented.

I CAN'T STAND UP
FOR FALLING DOWN
ELVIS COSTELLO (1980)
Original by Sam and Dave (1967)

Get Happy!!, Elvis Costello and the Attractions' 1980 retro-soul inspired album, contains two great covers: the punchy 'I Stand Accused', which Costello learned from the Merseybeats, and 'I Can't Stand up for Falling Down', which was written by Homer Banks and Allen Jones for Sam and Dave. A slow-shuffle number, the kind that might get spun as the disco is cooling down for the night, 'I Can't Stand Up' was originally the B-side to a 1967 Stax single, 'Soothe Me'. Costello found it amongst a handful of vintage soul seven-inches he had picked up from a record store, bought as homework for the album sessions.

Costello and the Attractions take Sam and Dave's ballad, and wind it up until it's sprung tighter than a Wigan dancefloor. It was recorded at Wisseloord Studios, in Hilversum, the Netherlands. "Wisseloord was a more sedate environment than we were used to," recalled Costello, "but it did have unforeseen advantages." Among these was the glass "strings" booth. "[That] proved to be most useful for creating the vocal sound on 'I Can't Stand Up'," he said.

When Radar Records, Costello's late-Seventies label, folded, the single release of 'I Can't Stand Up' was slated for Jerry Dammers' 2-Tone label – home to the Specials, whom Costello had recently produced. After some legal wrangling it instead appeared on a new imprint, F-Beat, and copies of the 2-Tone pressing were disposed of at gigs.

The B-side, 'Girl's Talk', was itself a huge hit in the capable hands of Dave Edmunds. "Perhaps I was careless to give this song away," said Costello. As covers go though, it seems a fair swap.

PROMISED LAND
JOHNNIE ALLAN (1971)
Original by Chuck Berry (1964)

Elvis Presley cut a version in 1973, but the best rendition of Chuck Berry's 'Promised Land' is the 1971 cover by Cajun pop star Johnnie Allan. So good is this non-hit that it has since appeared on over 30 compilations.

Never mind Johnny B. Goode, the real Chuck Berry hero is the anonymous "poor boy" who straddles a Greyhound out of Norfolk, Virginia with California on his mind. In around two minutes, Chuck drives his ever-resourceful alter-ego coast-to-coast through a dozen states, by bus, train and plane, roaming ever westwards, from Raleigh to Rock Hill, Georgia to the Golden State, with barely a moment to take in a breath, let alone the view. If one could accompany any character from song, Sancho Panza-like, who would refuse a trip with Berry's poor boy?

Like 'Route 66' or Simon and Garfunkel's 'America', 'Promised Land' is rock 'n' roll cartography, plotting a line through pop's musical heartland. Berry wrote it in a midwest prison and it was recorded, on his release, at Chess studios in Chicago in 1964. One who was there was the late Guy Stevens - in the Seventies a noteworthy producer of acts such as the Clash, but in 1964 a journalist for *Jazz Beat* magazine. "One of the undoubted highlights of my recent American visit turned out be the Chuck Berry recording session which I sat in on," he wrote, diligently noting that the session took place on Thursday, 20 February, commencing at approximately 6pm. The first number out of the bag was 'Promised Land'. Berry supervised the musicians: Willie Dixon on bass, Ellis Leake on piano, plus some un-named backup boys. Chuck kicked off with a killer chord and sang the lyrics from his own music sheets. "The rest of the musicians soon fell in with him," reported Stevens.

Behind the glass sat the producer Phil Chess, his fingers on the dials, a smile on his face. Berry's song clearly tickled those present: "It turned out to be so amusing that the studio engineers and Phil Chess himself frequently grinned and laughed during the recording," says Stevens. "We then all piled into the control room to hear the playbacks... Chess seemed very pleased with the results, especially on 'Promised Land', and indicated that it could well he Chuck's next single release." After cutting his cover, Allan wrote to Berry to tell him all about it, but he was disappointed: "All I wanted was for him to send me an autographed picture," he reported. "But I never heard from him."

(THEY LONG TO BE) CLOSE TO YOU
BOBBY WOMACK (1971)
Original by Richard Chamberlain (1963)

Things weren't looking too good for Burt Bacharach and Hal David's new song in 1963. First off, it was a non-hit for the actor, singer and all-round teen idol Richard Chamberlain. Starting out as an A-side, Chamberlain's original was swiftly overtaken by its B-side, 'Blue Guitar'. Dusty Springfield demoed a version in 1964 which took three years to make it to vinyl. Then it was covered by Dionne Warwick, winding up as a largely ignored flip-side to her 1965 single 'Here I am'. The public just weren't ready for 'Close to You'.

When A&M label manager and trumpeter Herb Alpert brought it to Richard Carpenter in early 1970, Carpenter wasn't so sure either. "Herbie said, 'I have a record, but I don't want you to hear it'," Carpenter said, recalling how wary Alpert was of the previous flop recordings influencing his arrangement. Alpert insisted on just one thing – that after the first bridge there were two five-note arpeggios on the piano, "one, and then another, down an octave". Carpenter complied with Alpert's request and the two spent several studio hours collaborating on their arrangement. The result was A&M's biggest seller for two years. Those double-octave quintuplets and Karen Carpenter's sumptuous "Wah", which filled the song's coda, were the hooks. Their hit defined the duo's lush sound and beat the Beatles and Simon and Garfunkel to a Grammy for Best Contemporary Vocal Performance in 1970.

With 'Close to You' finally and firmly established as a classic, other artists jumped on it, from Diana Ross in the Seventies to the Cranberries in the Nineties and Paul Weller in the twenty-first century. The most moving is Bobby Womack's nine-minute version, recorded for the 1971 album *Communication* – one of the era's overlooked gems. Womack prefaces his cover with a confessional rap, in which he bemoans the pressure he suffered by record bosses, urging him to "sell out" in order to stay in contract ("We like you, but you're not commercial..."). Poor Bobby? Not a bit of it – 'Close to You' is his riposte to a music business that squeezed and squashed the Womack sound to fit the balance sheet: "Now I wanna sing something that *I* wanna sing!" he declares before launching into the most proudly soulful version of Bacharach and David.

BABY I LOVE YOU
THE RAMONES (1979)
Original by the Ronnettes (1963)

It was as easy as 1-2-3-4. Ok, it was a little slower than their usual material, but surely 'Baby I Love You' was tailor-made for the Ramones. It all could have ended so horribly, however. According to Joey Ramone, the first thing Phil Spector said when he met them was, "My bodyguards want to fight your bodyguards." Joey was taken aback and told Spector that they didn't have any bodyguards. When da brudders bumped into him again at a Blondie gig in 1978, Dee Dee Ramone remembers that Spector was wearing a batwing cape and aviator specs. "This man I can only describe as resembling Count Dracula himself," said Dee Dee.

Spector and the Ramones eventually found themselves in the same studio – Gold Star in LA, Spector's usual place of work – and working on an album. Tensions were soon running high, however, and Dee Dee threatened to walk. In an incident at Spector's home, which has gone down in rock 'n' roll myth, the errant producer pulled a shooter on the bassist. "He leveled the gun at my heart, then motioned for me and the rest of the band to get back in the piano room," said Dee Dee. When they were all sitting quietly again Spector made everyone listen to him play 'Baby I Love You' until 4.30 the following morning.

The song was of course originally a hit for the Ronettes. In truth it was only the 15-year-old Ronnie Bennett, Spector's wife to be, on lead vocals when it was recorded at the end of 1963, while the other Ronettes were off touring. Amongst the backing singers was a pre-famous Cher. A love letter in song, it was penned by the husband-and-wife team of Ellie Greenwich and Jeff Barry and took over 40 takes to get right. It also charted in a soundalike cover by Dave Edmunds, in 1973.

Spector's insistence that the Ramones record a version of the

15-year-old song with him was not popular with the group. Eventually Spector, who was unused to working with bands, singled out Joey Ramone and brought in some of his usual session men to fill the others' shoes. "It didn't sound anything like the Ramones," said Joey. There was talk of releasing the cover as a solo Joey single, but the band mentality was too strong and it wound up on the Ramones' album *End of the Century* – a title supplied by Spector. Released as a single it was, ironically, the Ramones' biggest chart success and Spector's last great contribution to rock 'n' roll.

BONUS TRACK

SMELLS LIKE TEEN SPIRIT
TORI AMOS (1992)
Original by Nirvana (1991)

At the last count there were well over 200 covers of Nirvana's signature tune on Spotify – and that's just scratching the surface. 'Smells Like Teen Spirit' is one of the most covered songs of the last 25 years. You may prefer the Muppet Barbershop Quartet's a cappella version to Paul Anka's swing-along, or Pimpi Arroyo's chilled-out lounge arrangement to those by MGMT, Take That or Bruno Mars – or Miley Cyrus, who cited the song as one of the reasons she decided to become a performer. The truth is 'Teen Spirit' can be slowed down, up-tempo'd, or shaken into pretty much any genre you like. Somehow, it still works.

An early cover of the grunge anthem was from Steinway siren Tori Amos, whose beetle-browed arrangement appeared on the 1992 EP *Crucify*. Amos first came across the song in Sweden. She'd never heard of Nirvana but, watching the Seattle band on television, she had an idea. "When I heard it the first time the piano said to me, 'I want to do this', and when the piano tells me it wants to do something, she rules the roost." Kurt Cobain was flattered. It quickly became his and Courtney Love's wake-up call. "We used to put it on every morning and have breakfast and dance around," Cobain commented. "We'd turn it up really loud and do interpretive dancing to it. It's good breakfast music."

The song had already come a long way, in under a year. Originally begun by Cobain, in an attempt to pastiche the Pixies, one of the bands he admired, and founded on a guitar chop by prog-rockers Boston, 'Teen Spirit' ended up a band effort, after the guitarist bludgeoned his band mates with the riff for an hour-and-a-half. The title came about after Cobain's friend Kathleen Hanna had sprayed "Kurt smells like Teen Spirit" on his wall. Unaware that Teen Spirit was in fact a brand of deodorant worn by this then girlfriend, Cobain read revolutionary meaning into the innocuous slogan. An initial draft of the song was sent to Nirvana's producer, Butch Vig, in 1990. It was recorded at California's Sound City in May 1991 and unleashed on an unsuspecting public four months later. No one figured it would be a hit ('Come As You Are' was initially earmarked as the likely crossover song), but thanks to MTV, college radio and public adulation, the buzz gradually became a roar.

Since Amos, it's been tackled by everyone from buskers to boy bands. Founding punk Patti Smith included a suitably reverential tribute on her 2007 album of covers, *Twelve*, alongside reworkings of songs by REM, Neil Young and the Doors. If 'Smells Like Teen Spirit' is America's "Anarchy in the UK", then it is appropriate, perhaps, that the song's "Hello, hello, hello…" hook echoes Public Image's eponymous debut. It even found a reluctant fan in John Lydon: "Well, I've seen it like this: Nevermind Without the Bollocks," he said, of the song's parent album. "But 'Smells Like Teen Spirit' was stunning."